SAN JUAN SAMPLER

Selections from the Nina Heald Webber
Southwest Colorado Postcard Collection

ISBN 1-887805-11-7

Editor
Andrew Gulliford

Authors
Lynne R. Carpenter
Art Goodtimes
Ann Hoffman
Nik Kendziorski
Richard Moe
Freda Peterson
Bev Rich
Duane Smith
Nina Webber

Design and Layout
Lisa Snider Atchison

Durango Herald Small Press
P.O. Drawer A, Durango, Colorado 81302
email: dhsp@frontier.net
Order at: www.theheraldstore.com
or call toll free: 1-800-530-8318 Ext. 4585

Center of Southwest Studies
Fort Lewis College
1000 Rim Drive
Durango, Colorado 81301
970-247-7456
swcenter.fortlewis.edu

Dedicated to those who honor, enjoy,
and remember the past,
and to those who have preserved
memories for the future.

CONTENTS

Top: Rocky Point, along the old Ouray-Silverton Stage Road. Today, locals and tourists know this section of road as the Million Dollar Highway.

Far left:: Wilson Peak rises over 14,000 feet above a picturesque ranch near Telluride, Colorado.

FOREWORD

From an early age, collecting was part of my life. My grandparents, uncles, aunts, cousins, and, most importantly, my parents, all collected. For me collecting marbles came first, followed by a collection of small decorative pitchers, then collections of jokers from playing cards, which led the way to collecting more "grownup" objects such as 18th and 19th century samplers. However, it wasn't until the early 1980s that I became aware of postcard collecting. My sister-in-law sent me a thank-you note on a postcard which I proudly framed. This was not just any postcard, but one that showed the peninsula where we summered. This started my interest in collecting postcards.

"THE THRILL OF THE HUNT IS SO APPEALING! WHY ELSE WOULD I BE UP AT 5:00 A.M., DRIVING THREE OR MORE HOURS TO A POSTCARD SHOW?"

A local antiques dealer introduced me to postcards of our little town in Massachusetts, and suggested other dealers and contacts from whom I might buy local postcards. A defining moment in my postcard collecting occurred when I spied a card showing the summer house in which I grew up, a postcard printed in the early 1900s showing our residence with a horse and buggy in front of the house. I knew I was hooked. And for almost twenty-five years, I have made collecting postcards, ephemera, and souvenir china my main hobbies. From just one area of Massachusetts, I have expanded my collection to over 35 geographic areas, each of which has touched my life or that of my family.

The thrill of the hunt is so appealing! Why else would I be up at 5:00 a.m., driving three or more hours to a postcard show? Talking "shop" with dealers, hearing tales of local history, meeting interesting collectors and dealers from all walks of life and from all over the United States is the icing on the cake of collecting.

People often ask me where I find my collectibles. Of course, you would expect to find collectibles in flea markets, multi-dealer shops, antique shops, stamp and coin dealers (they often have postcards as a sideline), but the real fun is at the regional postcard and ephemera shows where, in some cases, close to one hundred dealers attend. Exhausting to be sure, but exhilarating, and one can really unearth great finds. Also, friends breaking up a parent's or relative's home call me to see if the shoe box of postcards they've discovered has any value. It is an honor and a pleasure to see these, and to give them my amateur's opinion as to where the postcards might be properly evaluated and, if desired, sold.

The real satisfaction has been to create or add to historical collections at secondary schools, colleges, historical societies and museums. Learning how to preserve, organize and display postcards has been fascinating. It is very important to me that my various collections be made available to the public, whether for research, investigation or simply to entertain those wanting to see what their town looked like ninety years ago. What started for me as a hobby has become a means to share with the public my "windows to the past," which are priceless memories of previous eras. I do hope readers enjoy seeing these mementos as much as I have enjoyed collecting them.

— Nina Heald Webber

Early postcard of the agricultural town of Animas City. In the 1870s, the town was a supply center for the mines sprouting up in the San Juan Mountains near Silverton. When the Denver & Rio Grande Railroad arrived Animas City turned down their offers to be a railroad center. Thus, in 1880 the railroad created the town of Durango which annexed Animas City in 1947.

INTRODUCTION

This marvelous postcard book about small towns in the western San Juans, and the spectacular Million Dollar Highway that connects them, is one of numerous special projects, exhibits, and archival acquisitions for the 40th anniversary of the Center of Southwest Studies at Fort Lewis College in Durango, Colorado. As with many of our collections, we are deeply indebted to donors for making this possible, specifically Nina Heald Webber, and to researchers and writers who have given their time to tell the story of the small towns of Durango, Silverton, Ouray and Telluride. Ms. Webber's gift of over 2,300 historic postcards and her financial support has made this book a reality.

In the 1890s the San Juan Mountains represented the Silicon Valley of the 19th century because Eastern capital flowed into these remote mountain valleys as prospectors searched for and discovered rich veins of silver and gold. The wealth of the mountains and the wealth of investors brought rapid increases in technology to hard rock mining. The first long distance transmission of alternating current in the world occurred near Telluride thanks to L.L. Nunn. Other industrial achievements included development of aerial tram systems, which helped to make the ski industry successful around the world, and the Wilfley Table that effectively sorted gold from other minerals.

The San Juan Mountains boomed at the end of the 19th century, but the last and best year for Silverton was 1910 when San Juan County, Colorado, had 3,000 people. Now there are 600 citizens in town and 3,000 in the cemetery. Despite sporadic attempts to revive mining, by 1952 when the Ballantine family from New York and Minnesota bought *The Durango Herald*, mining had greatly diminished. The Ballantines understood the natural beauty of the area and like so many other families from the East and Midwest, they took a gamble on southwestern Colorado. They became committed to the local communities and fledgling Fort Lewis College.

By 1964 the college had moved into town from its original location and had evolved from a two-year institution into a four-year baccalaureate degree-granting public liberal arts college. Arthur Ballantine, publisher of *The Durango Herald*, asked what he could do to help give the new four-year college academic distinction. The decision was to create a Center of Southwest Studies, so in 1964 Arthur and Morley Ballantine donated the first $10,000 to start the center.

Million Dollar Highway

An omnibus is entered in a parade. The omnibus was an urban taxi that was used in Silverton to take railroad passengers from the depot to the Grand Imperial Hotel. In 1937, the omnibus was restored and entered into Durango's Spanish Trails Fiesta Days Parade by Harry Jackson, a local hardware store and carriage shop owner. The omnibus was a regular entrant in the parade and became a symbol of the Fiesta Days until the 1960s. After a century it is now back in Silverton on display at the San Juan County Historical Society's Mining Heritage Center.

Early postcard of autos on the Million Dollar Highway. Notice the stone guard walls that kept motorists from getting too close to the steep cliffs. Stone guard walls like those pictured can still be seen on a section of the Old Lime Creek Road.

Forty years later, Fort Lewis College has the oldest academic center in the nation dedicated to preserving, documenting, and interpreting the Southwest. The Center of Southwest Studies began as a single room in the college administration building and then moved to the top floor of Reed Library where the Arthur Ballantine Reading Room housed its collection of major books, articles, microfilm, and primary source documents essential to studying the Southwest. The facility worked fine for research, but it was too small for public programming. Then in January of 2001 we moved into a new 48,000 square foot, $8 million building that provides a 100+ seat lyceum, a 4,400-square-foot gallery and a 2,200-square foot research library and archives. A large segment of our collection documents the mining towns of the San Juans and the brave men and women who brought their dreams west in the 19th century.

We work with donors, researchers and writers from around the nation who visit us personally in Durango or who visit us on the World Wide Web. Two decades later we still have excellent relations with the Ballantine family, and it is with great satisfaction that on the center's 40th anniversary we publish with the Durango Herald Small Press *A San Juan Sampler: Selections from the Nina Heald Webber Southwest Colorado Postcard Collection*.

"THE MOUNTAIN TOWNS OF THE SAN JUANS REPRESENT THAT PERFECT INTERSECTION BETWEEN THE PAST AND THE FUTURE... ."

These essays have been written by researchers and top scholars in their local communities as well as by Richard Moe, president of the National Trust for Historic Preservation and a summer resident of Ophir, Colorado. Ophir lies just around the corner from Telluride and a mountain pass away from Silverton. The small towns featured in these essays and postcards have survived because of the grit and determination of their residents. Though the hard rock mining industry is gone, and for environmental reasons will not return, the towns are doing well. Housing prices have skyrocketed and these small communities in the heart of the San Juans have been "discovered" by both summer and winter visitors who are equity émigrés and modern cowboys moving to the Rockies and the New West.

Once written off because of their isolation, the magnificent setting of these communities is now their greatest asset. The mines have closed but unparalleled mountain recreation, access to the high peaks of the San Juans, and some of the cleanest air in the country, make these communities viable and vibrant 21st century magnets for skiers, snowboarders, ice climbers, mountain climbers, mountain bikers and active retirees. In a speech to the Ouray County Historical Society in August 2002, Richard Moe of the National Trust for Historic Preservation discussed how visitors "will not go to a community that has lost its soul." He said, "People are yearning for a connectedness with the past and with what is real." The mountain towns of the San Juans represent that perfect intersection between the past and the future with plenty of nearby 13,000-foot mountain peaks, wilderness areas, national forests, and adjacent national monuments and parks.

The towns of Ouray, Durango, Silverton, and Telluride have protected their past and preserved their architecture. Each of the communities has National Historic Register districts, and Silverton has no less than three National Historic Landmarks — the town, the Mayflower Mill, and the famous Durango & Silverton Narrow Gauge Railroad, which has brought tourists to Silverton each summer for over a century.

In *San Juan Sampler*, Ann Hoffman writes about her hometown of Ouray, Bev Rich (born in the Silverton Miners Hospital) and Freda Peterson write about Silverton, and the eminent historian Dr. Duane Smith (who has written over 30 books) writes about Durango. San Miguel County Commissioner and environmental activist Art Goodtimes writes about Telluride. Public historian Nik Kendziorski writes about the Million Dollar Highway with references to the San Juan Skyway and the Red Mountain Project. The Red Mountain Task Force, partnering with the Trust for Public Land, is preserving the mountain landscape by purchasing mining claims from willing sellers to place private land back into the public domain. A century after settlement, the mountains remain rugged and wild. The Million Dollar Highway is crossed by sixty avalanche paths between Cascade Creek and Ouray, yet the Colorado Department of Transportation keeps it open year. *San Juan Sampler* concludes with essays by Lynne Carpenter and Todd Ellison, who give us a perspective on postcards.

Much has happened in the silvery San Juans since the Baker Expedition came into the upper valleys of the Animas River in 1860. With energy and optimism, prospectors and promoters established log cabin mining camps, but often those tiny communities failed because of fire, avalanches, and the decline of mineral production. Eureka, Gladstone, Chattanooga, Ironton, Animas Forks, Red Mountain and Gunston are no more, but Telluride, Durango, Silverton and Ouray survived and now thrive. Enjoy these essays and the accompanying historic postcards and learn why so many of us are proud to call these mountain towns our home.

— **Andrew Gulliford**
Director
Center of Southwest Studies

PREFACE:
CONNECTING TO THE PAST

During the past several years as a part-time resident of Ophir, I've had the good fortune to spend a fairly significant amount of time in southwestern Colorado. I've found that this place, perhaps more than any other I've known, is able to provide just about anything I want or need: relaxation, adventure, contemplation, discovery, even healing. That's one of the major reasons why I've joined thousands of other people, residents and visitors alike, in concluding that this is quite simply one of the best places on earth.

What is it that makes this part of the world so special? The scenery is spectacular, of course, and the climate is fine and the people are friendly, but there's more to the San Juans than alpine vistas and good weather and smiling faces. A truly special place is one that makes us feel personally connected to it in a meaningful way. For me — and, I suspect, for many other people as well — that feeling of connectedness is rooted in a sense of history. It's hard to feel connected to Noplace; fortunately for all of us, a strong sense of the past is one of the characteristics that identifies southwestern Colorado as Someplace.

This region of mountains and mesas, forest and grassland, has a rich history stretching back over thousands of years and involving some prominent players in the American saga, ranging from Ancestral Puebloan peoples to mining-era millionaires, from the ragged prospectors of the 19th century to the flashy skiers and snowboarders of today. This history is embodied in an incredibly diverse collection of historic structures and landscapes, from 19th-century hotels and storefronts to the ruins of Mesa Verde and the new Canyons of the Ancients National Monument. These places are a tremendous resource for anyone who wants to learn something about the history of this marvelous pocket of the American West. You could learn about it from books, certainly, but *reading* history can't compare with the experience of *walking through* history, seeing in the bricks and boards of old buildings — or the cliff dwellings and kivas of ancient canyons — a tangible expression of the dreams and achievements of people long dead, an entryway into our nation's collective memory.

What's more — and this may be the best news of all — the region has a strong and growing preservation consciousness. Years ago, visionary preservationists banded together to save the Durango & Silverton Narrow Gauge Railroad and a wealth of

The small post office of Ophir, Colorado, also may have doubled as the local gas station.

A steam train enters the railroad depot in the small mining town of Ophir, Colorado. Ophir is south of Telluride and is most famous for the engineering of a railroad loop. The Ophir Loop was a series of trestles and tight turns on the Rio Grande Southern route.

The Beaumont Hotel opened in 1887 and was instantly one of the grand hotels of Colorado. It rivaled Denver's Brown Palace Hotel.

The famous Cliff Palace of Mesa Verde National Park seen by the Wetherill brothers in 1888.

historic buildings in towns like Ouray and Telluride. The National Trust has presented National Preservation Honor Awards to the San Juan County Historical Society and the town of Silverton for their restoration of the Silverton Town Hall after a devastating fire; to Dan and Mary King for their hands-on commitment to the rebirth of Ouray's Beaumont Hotel; and to the Ute Mountain Tribal Park for its work in preserving and interpreting ancient structures and artworks that are world-class treasures. All over the area, private citizens and elected officials have developed successful public-private partnerships that utilize preservation as an engine for bolstering the local economy. And the work of organizations like Crow Canyon Archaeological Center have provided a model for the protection and preservation of priceless archaeological resources so that future generations will be able to appreciate and learn from them.

That's quite a record of accomplishment. It calls to mind a statement by anthropologist Margaret Mead: "Never doubt that a small group of thoughtful, committed individuals can change the world; indeed, it is the only thing that ever has."

I'm very proud of the National Trust's role in assisting the grass-roots efforts that have successfully preserved so much of the San Juans' heritage. We've provided financial support for several projects over the years, and our Mountains/Plains Office in Denver has offered advice, information and hands-on help as well. In addition to using our awards to spotlight local examples of preservation at its best, we've also included several sites in the region on our annual list of America's 11 Most Endangered Historic Places. Mesa Verde National Park, for example, appeared on the 1998 list because chronically inadequate funding was preventing the National Park Service from stabilizing and maintaining scores of significant sites in the park. A year after the list was announced, Mesa Verde was named an official project of Save America's Treasures. Congress appropriated funds to help meet the backlog of critical needs at the park, and private donors provided generous gifts to match the federal dollars. Mesa Verde isn't "saved" — not by a long shot — but some steps in the right direction have been taken.

Unfortunately, merely designating a site "endangered" doesn't guarantee a dramatic victory. Soon after the Red Mountain Mining District appeared on our endangered list in 2000, a landowner in Ouray County demolished several historic structures in the area. That hurts, especially when it happens for no good reason — and what makes this kind of preservation defeat especially tragic is the fact that when we lose a historic place, it's gone *forever*.

Small-town storefronts and battlefields, ancient ruins and roadside drive-ins, presidential estates and miners' shacks — they all tell America's story. They delight the eye and nourish the spirit. They help us know who we are and how we got here. They enrich our environment and our lives. They are, in short, incredibly important to us as a nation and as individuals. They're much too important to be lost.

I don't know who said this, but it's absolutely right: *"In the end, we will conserve only what we love, we will love only what we understand, and we will understand only what we are taught."* I do know who said this, because it's the tagline of a national media campaign that the National Trust is currently conducting: *"History is in our hands."*

"...THERE SHOULD BE, IN EVERY LIFE, A PLACE...WHERE YOU COULD COME AND VISIT YOUR PAST, AND THE PAST OF YOUR PEOPLE, AND KNOW THAT WHATEVER HAPPENED OUTSIDE, HERE TIMELESSNESS LIVED."

With those two statements in mind, our challenge is clear: We must keep teaching people that our heritage is too important to be hauled off to the landfill. We must keep sounding the alarm bell, alerting people to the threats that can let familiar landmarks go up in a cloud of smoke or collapse in a cloud of dust. Perhaps most important, we must keep reminding ourselves that saving our historic treasures isn't someone else's responsibility.

What does all of this have to do with the postcards pictured in this book?

Like the region they depict, these images from the Nina Heald Webber collection are a great source of entertainment and enlightenment, offering some surprises, a hefty dose of nostalgia and maybe even a few laughs. But they are something else as well. As Andrew Gulliford implies in his Introduction, they are vivid windows on the past — and that gives them an importance far beyond their inherent value as old scraps of cardboard.

In many cases, the places pictured here — towns, dusty roads, valleys and mountainsides — have changed dramatically since they were photographed. Happily, the Ophir Post Office still exists, although the gas pump shown next to it is long gone. Other places seen on these pages, especially the buildings — houses, railroad stations, stores and mining structures — have disappeared completely, leaving us only these pictures as mementos of their existence.

The Knife Edge Road was an early section of the entrance road into Mesa Verde National Park. This section of road is no longer used, but visitors can still follow much of its route as a hiking trail.

Spruce Tree Camp in the late 1910s was the park headquarters and main starting point for visitors in Mesa Verde National Park. Such primitive conditions were replaced when the Civilian Conservation Corps built more modern buildings and visitor services in the early 1930s. Today, there is also a modern hotel located in the park.

608. KNIFE EDGE ROAD, MESA VERDE NATIONAL PARK, COLORADO.

117632

MAIN AVENUE, NORTH FROM EIGHTH STREET.   DURANGO, COLORADO.

Main Avenue of Durango, Colorado, looking north from Eighth Street. Notice the streetcar tracks running down the center of the street. The popularity of the automobile would soon make the streetcar line obsolete.

Large residence at the corner of 8th and 4th Avenues in Durango, Colorado.

Residence Section, cor. 8th and 4th Aves., Durango, Colo.
J. O. Taylor, Pub.

In other words, the images on these postcards, whether pretty or gritty, familiar or strange, are a warning. Our legacy from the past is important, but it's also fragile. We need it, but we can lose it. Sturdy old buildings get torn down. Beautiful valleys get paved over. Places we care about turn into places we don't even recognize. Someplace turns into Anyplace, and eventually it becomes Noplace. It's happening everywhere — and if we let it, it'll happen here.

Many readers in the San Juans, like millions of their counterparts all over the country, are familiar with the work of the Southern novelist Anne Rivers Siddons. One of her best-sellers contains this passage: "...there should be, in every life, a place...where you could come and visit your past, and the past of your people, and know that whatever happened outside, here timelessness lived."

She's right. All of us, whether we realize it or not, whether we call ourselves preservationists or not, need a place like that — a place where we can have our history close at hand, where we can see it, touch it, learn from it, be shaped and inspired by it.

If we preservationists — and I'm including everyone in that "we" — if we do our job well, that timelessness will live here in southwestern Colorado and in every community in America.

— **Richard Moe**
President, National Trust for Historic Preservation

The Smuggler Union Mills near Telluride, Colorado. Numerous industrialized mining sites like the Smuggler Union dotted the high country of the San Juan Mountains.

Smuggler Union Mills, Telluride, Colo.

DURANGO

———◦◦◦———

Durango is a Basque word with a variety of meanings from
watering place to valley with a river running through it.
There is a Durango, Mexico, which is our sister city,
and a Durango, Spain.

DURANGO AND ANIMAS RIVER VALLEY, COLO.

Sanborn
W-1836

BUCKING STEER AT SPANISH TRAILS FIESTA, DURANGO, COLO.

Sanborn
W-2219

Top left: Early view of Durango and the Animas River Valley.

Top right: Crowds fill the grandstand to watch bull riding at the Spanish Trails Fiesta in Durango, Colorado. The Fiesta started in the mid 1930s and was meant to be a "true show of the west" and entertain tourists and locals of the San Juan Basin.

Right: Main Avenue looking north in Durango, Colorado. The automobile has taken over the street and the streetcar tracks have been removed.

THE QUINTESSENTIAL WESTERN TOWN

BY DUANE SMITH

Durango, the name sounds western and the town is western. Nestled in the Animas Valley where for more than two thousand years people have hunted, farmed, and lived, Durango has a fascinating heritage.

If one could have been a Rip Van Winkle and alternated naps with up and about periods, he or she could have seen the epic of the entire American West pass. First came the Ancestral Puebloan people, followed by the Utes, Spanish explorers, multinational fur trappers, and then Americans. By 1860, miners on their way to the San Juans hastened through, then a decade later came permanent settlement with ranchers, farmers, and their tiny village, Animas City. Soon the army appeared, followed by town builders, railroad and smelter workers, tourists, health seekers, coal miners, and in the midst of all this, Durango.

Named after Durango, Mexico, that in turn was named after Durango, Spain, the Denver & Rio Grande Railroad gave it birth. Durango is a Basque word with a variety of meanings from watering place to valley with a river running through it.

The river, the Animas, has been the key to all that has happened in this valley. Located in, at best a semi-arid region, the river provided a green oasis furnishing the staples of life that allowed settlement to plant roots from the very start of human arrival. In the 1870s, the glitter of gold and silver north in the San Juan Mountains lured prospectors and miners to "get rich without working." They needed beef, oats, and vegetables, however, the mountains offered a growing season that lasted at best twenty or so days. Thus, settlers came where there existed a hundred day growing season, water, and rich river bottom land. They called their little settlement Animas City.

The railroad then appeared, chugging up the valley to tap those camps high in the mountains. The Denver & Rio Grande would have made Animas City the railroad hub, but the city fathers would not meet their terms. So the railroad did what it had done before, started its own town. Thus Durango was born on September 13, 1880, two miles south of its older neighbor. Animas City survived awhile longer, but finally in 1947, it voted to join Durango.

Within an amazingly short time, Durango became the transportation, banking, business, and social hub of southwestern Colorado. It grew quickly topping 2,000 residents by the time of its first Christmas and according to the 1890 census count 2,700.

Overlooking the Animas River as it winds down the valley toward Durango, Colorado.

The Denver & Rio Grande Railroad created the town of Durango and it is the narrow gauge railroad that continues to be one of the town's main tourist attractions. Engine 315 sits on display in Durango, Colorado.

An early view of Durango. The large pine tree at the center of the postcard is where Henry Moorman was lynched for murder. Like many early railroad towns, there was a period of "lawlessness" that eventually settled down and gave rise to a "civilized" town.

The "magic metropolis," among the names it called itself, lived up to that reputation.

Durangoans tried their best to recreate the life they left behind and establish Victorian America along the curve of the Animas River. Overall they succeeded. That legendary, really fictional, wild West found no home here. If for no other reason, that image would have been bad for business and growth. After all to this generation, and others as well, it was "grow or die." Having a "man for breakfast," as the saying went, or a "wild" birth, would not enhance what these people really wanted — investors, settlers, and a reputation as a progressive community.

Conversely, it also sported a pair of red-light districts with their saloons, gambling "hells," cribs, and parlor houses. They were good for business in the male dominated world of mining, ranching, and railroading. To appease Victorian sensibilities and ease the tax load on local pocketbooks, the city council passed ordinances against such activities, then city government routinely collected their monthly fines.

"IN THE END, THE VISION OF THE DENVER & RIO GRANDE PROMOTERS HAD BEEN RIGHT. THEIR "METROPOLIS" COMMANDED ALL WITHIN ITS GRASP."

This clash of morality vs. practicality happened throughout the West. Without the red-light districts, potential customers went elsewhere, a thought which startled the business community. Fascinating, such "sin" also intrigued visitors who had little such opportunities in their hometowns or feared public condemnation if they indulged.

Durango was blessed with advantages that its neighbors often did not possess: its beautiful location, its climate, a good water supply, fertile land, natural resources, hot springs for health seekers and an abundance of "movers and shakers" to promote it all. Typically however, for the era, it got into nasty little scrapes with its neighbors. Nineteenth and early twentieth century urban rivalries were no holds barred in the struggle to gain local and regional supremacy.

Before it was all over, Durango dominated. Animas City did not stand a chance. Silverton, at the north end of the railroad, relied on its mining and when that

Smoke drifts over Durango from its largest industry, smelters processing ore from mines in the San Juan Mountains. In the early 1900s, Durango had grown to include schools, churches, smelters and permanent residences.

boomed the community prospered, but when mining fell, Silverton slipped into the doldrums. To the west, Cortez never gained the railroad (every community worth "its salt" had to have railroad connections) and thus started off slowly and failed to catch up with its rival. Parrott City lost the county seat to Durango and eventually gained only ghost town status. Mancos, Bayfield, and Ignacio spit and hissed at their larger neighbor without much impact. They based their economies on agriculture and stumbled along with it. In the end, the vision of the Denver & Rio Grande promoters had been right. Their "metropolis" commanded all within its grasp.

Upstart, youthful Durango also took on Denver and Leadville, then Colorado's silver queen, but did not do so well in either case. In fact, it took on anyone who in some way challenged or threatened this "bound to boom" new town. Eventually matters quieted down, but always vigilant Durango and its business community never let their guard slip.

Speaking of Parrott City, that little mining camp at the mouth of La Plata Canyon had been the county seat before Durango burst on the scene. Nothing added to a community's prestige and future than gaining that honor. Court sessions and county matters also brought visitors and money to the community. Durangoans were not ready to let that opportunity go unheeded. As a result they petitioned to have an election on the question of the county seat location.

There existed no question how the result would turn out. In November 1881, Durangoans overwhelmingly voted for their community and that decided the issue. Durango became the county seat, a designation it has retained. The no-holds barred, urban warfare of the nineteenth century took no prisoners. Eventually the town built a fine courthouse to accommodate county offices and add to the Durango skyline. It would finally be torn down in 1964. The old clock was saved and replaced in a new tower in 1989.

What made this all possible? Those movers and shakers parlayed every opportunity available to them. For example, coal deposits were found south, east, and west of town. The D&RG officials knew this and were first to take advantage of it. Steam engines needed coal, so did everyone else, thus a ready-made profitable business opportunity stood at the doorstep of their town.

Not only did coal mines flourish, Durango had three tiny satellite coal camps nearby — Porter, Hesperus, and Perins. It also seized the opportunity to open a smelter. Gold and silver, when mined from the earth, need to be refined to separate the precious metals from the waste rock. This was done in mills and smelters using various processes. Mining was carried on high in the San Juans, but smelters could be better operated where coal and better transportation were available. After all, hauling ore down a hill proved cheaper than to transport everything up a hill to the mines.

Besides those advantages, Durango's climate was milder than Silverton's and the

Looking south on Main Avenue as a parade makes its way through downtown Durango in the early 1900s. The pervasive smelter smoke meant full employment.

The La Plata County Courthouse and its fine clock tower. The courthouse was torn down in 1964, but the clock was saved and replaced in a new tower at a new courthouse in 1989.

town offered more opportunities. One should not imagine, though, that Durango basked in a tropical climate. Particularly in the nineteenth century, the winters could be difficult and travel hard even by train. Not infrequently, snowslides stopped trains going to Silverton and deep snow isolated farmers, ranchers, and town folk.

Durango secured a smelter by purchasing Silverton's and moving it south, much to Silvertonians' displeasure and dismay. The San Juan and New York smelter was blown in 1881, but did not hit full stride until the railroad reached Silverton in July of the next year. Finally, San Juan mining came of age.

The smelter passed through several owners before becoming part of the gigantic American Smelting and Refining Company. As such, it brought Durango into the turn-of-the-century world of big business and corporations. The predictable result occurred, Durango became the center of some labor unrest. That did not help the town's image, and unions and strikes were not welcome either at the smelter or in the coal mines.

Without question for a generation, the smelter remained Durango's most important business and its largest employer. Gold and silver, brought down from the mines, were crushed, heated, given chemical baths, and eventually freed to become glittering bars. The smoke, bellowing out of tall stacks spoke of progress and profit. It also smelled like rotten eggs and when gently pushed by the wind settled over the community. The noise of those stamps crushing the ore could be heard all the way to Animas City. Durangoans did not mind. The noise and smell denoted

Above: Large snow banks down Main Avenue in Durango in the 1930s. Today, such winter scenes are rare in Durango, though annual snowfall should average 60 inches.

Right: Narrow-gauge train clearing a snowslide from the tracks in the Animas River canyon. Heavy snowfall and large snowslides could prevent the train from reaching Silverton for days at a time.

NARROW GAUGE "BUCKING" SNOW SLIDE — ANIMAS CANYON, COLORADO

View of the large American Smelting and Refining Company complex along the Animas River in Durango. A large industrial complex was a sign of progress at the turn of the century.

American Smelting and Ref. Co., Durango, Colo.

5223

progress and coming of age industrially. Indeed, they enjoyed seeing that smoke hovering over their community and it appeared in photographs.

Equally significant to Durango's future was the fact that it emerged a railroad hub. Colorado's "Baby Railroad," the Denver & Rio Grande, gave it birth and a tremendous start. That proved just the start, however. Other railroads came and soon Durango had rails going in every direction.

In 1890-91, the Rio Grande Southern swung westward then northward around the San Juans. Along the way it tapped Mancos, created the town of Dolores, reached the mines at Rico, sent a spur line into Telluride, and established Ridgway where it again joined the D&RG. Its builder, Otto Mears, had great hopes, but the 1893 panic, and subsequent overwhelming depression, bankrupted his dream. The D&RG where it started and ended took it over; the company had also been a major stockholder in the venture.

The Rio Grande Southern, meanwhile, brought added prosperity to Durango. Ore from Rico and Telluride, until it gained its own mills, came over the line. A gateway to new towns, rural areas, and mining districts opened for Durango. The railroad would operate into the 1950s before it followed the path of many of its contemporaries into oblivion.

The Denver & Rio Grande found a new, profitable business, tourism to help shore up its profits. The "Swing Around the Circle" took visitors from Denver to Durango and on to Silverton and beyond. Eventually by stage, they could go to Ouray, reboard a train and venture back to Denver. Along the way, they saw some spectacular scenery, mining towns (with their image of a fast vanishing older West), and Ute Indians.

They could also see an older civilization, the remains of the first settlers of the region. Mancos gained mightily from the tourists on their way to see the ruins of the ancients, now Mesa Verde National Park. That only aroused Durango's jealousy and the two fought it out for a generation until guess who won!

Nevertheless, that was not all of Durango's railroads. Eventually a short line would run up to the coal camp of Perins and another, the "Red Apple," down through Aztec to Farmington, New Mexico. Durango had four lines connecting itself to the world beyond the Animas Valley.

These lines were all narrow gauge, except one, that was three feet between the rails as opposed to a standard gauge that was four foot eight and some half inches. The smaller gauge proved better for mountainous railroading. It cost less to build, could go around sharper curves, and could climb slightly steeper grades than its larger and more commonly used brother. Of course, a trade-off existed in all this. Narrow-gauge engines were smaller and less powerful and the cars could carry fewer

Smoke from the smelters rise above Main Avenue. The citizens of Durango did not mind the smoke because it represented prosperity. Today, the only smoke that rises above Main Avenue comes from the Durango & Silverton Narrow Gauge Railroad.

Narrow-gauge train at the Durango depot. Today, hundreds of thousands of tourists depart from this depot to make the trip to Silverton, Colorado, along the same route that was laid down in 1882.

DURANGO IS THE METROPOLIS OF THE SAN JUAN DISTRICT

OA5138

The reverse side of this postcard above states that Durango "is a modern city with fine conveniences and a population of nearly 6,000. It has fine hotels, tourist camps, a smelter, is a large railroad center, and a junction point on all highways in the Southwest section." Postcards were not just for depicting beautiful landscapes, but also for boosterism.

THE GALLOPING GOOSE AT DURANGO, COLO.

W-2102

passengers and freight. Isolated mountain mining towns did not mind, nor did Durango.

Interestingly, the one exception to this, the line to Farmington, was standard gauge. This, of course, caused problems of having to unload and reload cars. The reason for this inconvenience was to hold off competition coming from the south. The D&RG was prepared to build on, to stop the threat, however, it never materialized.

One of the more interesting railroad vehicles to travel in and out of Durango was the famed Galloping Goose. With traffic and revenue declining, the Rio Grande Southern, in the 1930s, converted some automobile bodies (several Buicks and Pierce Arrows bit the dust) into vehicles that could carry a few passengers and some light freight. Waddling along on the uneven trackage may have given them their nickname. Seven galloped at one time or another into the 1950s when the railroad ended its run. Restored, several geese live on. The rest have become the folklore of legend.

If one aspired to be a "major metropolis" in the nineteenth century, one had to have a "fancy" hotel. Here the investor, tourist, and potential settler could rest and relax, sleep in a bed with the "sheets cleaner than the wind driven snow," and enjoy a good cup of coffee. Denver had its Brown Palace, Central City its Teller House, and Durango its Strater Hotel.

Opened in August 1887, the Strater offered southwestern Colorado's finest accommodations. It, along with Durango's other hotels, boosted the town's image. Even at this early date, Durango offered the visiting public attractive stopping places.

Not that all Durangoans greeted the tourists with open arms. In the late 1880s, a local newspaper felt obligated, now that the spring season had arrived, to ask its readers to be pleasant to them! Why? If for no other reason, they brought in money.

One of the great attractions of the nineteenth century was mineral springs. Throughout the United States, they gained popularity in this day and time long before modern medicine. The various springs promised to cure everything from a sour stomach, to lost manhood, and even cancer.

Colorado benefited from its springs and also its "healthy" dry climate which contained lots of "ozone," a popular remedy. Durango marched right in step. It beckoned the weary and sick to come and rejuvenate themselves.

North up the Animas Valley were found a host of springs, the most famous Trimble Hot Springs. With the railroad running right by, and a short siding to park your private car, it awaited customers with a pool and mineral baths. For those who cared to ride their bicycles from town, a path existed for that. It also had a resort where they could have a Sunday dinner and a front lawn where a game of

Rio Grande Southern Railroad's Galloping Goose at the depot in Durango. From the 1930s until the 1950s these odd-looking vehicles were used to carry light freight, U.S. mail and a few passengers along the Rio Grande Southern route.

Trimble Hot Springs, near Durango, Colo.
J. O. Taylor, Pub.

Trimble Hot Springs drew many people to its "healing" waters and a fine resort was built to accommodate them. Unfortunately, two grand structures built at the hot springs burned down, including the one pictured in the postcard.

Strater Hotel, Durango, Colo.

The Strater Hotel opened its doors in 1887 and instantly boosted Durango's image. The Strater continues as one of Durango's most recognized buildings in its historic district.

The A. N. Knight Ranch in the Animas Valley north of Durango. The crops and livestock raised in the valley supplied the growing mining camps of the San Juan region and added to the economic diversity of Durango.

A.N. Knight's Ranch
Animas Valley

"Presbyterian billiards" helped pass away the afternoon; that meant croquet.

While riding in the valley, the farms, orchards, and ranches came into view. Durango and La Plata County always had a strong agricultural foundation. With water, fertile land, and a decent growing season, at least most years, crops and animals flourished.

Even better, a ready market existed in the mountain towns and mines, and once the D&RG arrived transporting goods northward became easy and economical. As a result, agriculture stepped to the forefront as one of the economic pillars of the town and country.

Actually, for a time, apple orchards gave the farmers a commercial crop, not only here but southward in New Mexico, hence the red apple nickname for the line running down there. Unfortunately, a fruit virus and the problems of shipment to a large market, i.e., Denver, eventually forced a cutback to local consumption.

Saturday was the day the farmers usually came to town, a good market day for local merchants. It might be a whole day's venture because the county roads would not improve beyond dirt and gravel until well into the twentieth century.

Finding a market beyond the region always presented a problem. Shipment to Denver was expensive and farmers and ranchers between here and there raised primarily the same things. They could ship them cheaper and the products arrived

The section of the D&RG R.R. Bridge that was washed away by the Animas R.

Top: A railroad car teeters on a section of a Denver & Rio Grande Railroad bridge that crossed the Animas River in Durango. The flood of 1911 washed away many bridges, large sections of track, flooded homes and left destruction in its wake. Many rivers in the San Juan Basin flooded that year.

Center: The reverse side of the postcard states, "The famous Diamond Belle in Durango's Strater Hotel. The fun spot of Durango's night-life, the 'Belle,' completely authentic early Western Americana, takes you back to those rollicking mining days at the turn of the century." Where the Diamond Belle is now was originally a pharmacy.

A parade entry by American Railway Express makes its way down Main Avenue in Durango.

1565 THE FAMOUS "MOVING MOUNTAIN" AT DURANGO, COLO.

VAY SOUTH OF DURANGO

3A184

GREETINGS FROM DURANGO, COLORADO

A135

Rena Haffley
Trick Rider
Durango 9-23-19

Left: The reverse states, "The 'Moving Mountain' is the latest wonder of the San Juan district and its peculiar actions have brought attention from all over the world. An immense section of the rocky strata that forms its top has split and broken away and it seems as if the whole mountain may eventually collapse." This "mountain" is a mass of disturbed rock on the east side of Carbon Mountain, south of Durango.

Far left: A smiling face and plenty of recreational opportunities welcome visitors to Durango.

Woman trick rider Rena Haffley displaying her skills in Durango on September 23, 1919.

A streetcar crosses the new city bridge over the Animas River in Durango. For a nickel, a rider could ride the entire 2-mile length of the line from the Durango depot to Animas City.

The Senior High School was built in 1916 and was a source of civic pride in Durango. Today, the building houses the District 9R Administration and has been listed on the National Register of Historic Places.

fresher. Even their one cash crop suffered. Apples unless extremely well packed suffered shifting and bruising, thereby being less appealing to the housewife or husband who was doing the shopping.

Meanwhile, back in town, Durango had come of age in another way. It had a trolley line running from the depot to Animas City. The Durango, Brookside (a subdivision) and Animas City trolley had another claim to fame — the country's shortest, franchised line. It was barely more than two miles.

For a nickel, the passenger could ride the whole distance. In the summertime, the sides were taken down and put back on when the winter winds blew. Young boys in town found that if they greased the tracks just north of the Main Avenue bridge, the trolley spun to a stop and might slide backward. The conductor then had to get out and clean the track while probably thinking some ill thoughts about the younger generation. Would Durango survive these hooligans?

❖ ❖ ❖

The question might be fairly asked, why were not the youngsters in school? They should have been. Durangoans from the start pushed education, after all schools improved the civic image. A good public school system would attract families and others and definitely benefited the community.

Durango quickly organized public schools, despite grumbling from some taxpayers. Then it added, what most of its neighbors did not have, a high school whose first principal was a woman, Sarah Scott Trew. By the 1890s, Durango could proudly point to its education system as one of the best outside of Denver.

Whether or not the youngsters appreciated those efforts may be questioned. It even pioneered in another area, women's athletics. Some high school girls, and the majority of the students at that level were feminine, pushed, after the turn of the century, for a basketball team. Following a long discussion, the school board finally granted their wish. However, only their parents and teachers could watch. Young men should not see the women cavorting about for it might raise their "base passions." That despite the fact that the uniforms genteelly covered the girls from ankle to neck.

Durango also had a Catholic private academy operated by the Sisters of Mercy. It advertised for young women throughout the region to come and finish their education. Located across the river in the new Fassbinder subdivision, it was in a complex with St. Columba church. All told, the school provided the proper religious, educational, and respectable atmosphere for young ladies.

The Sisters of Mercy also started and operated Durango's first hospital, also part of the complex. This, too, provided a drawing card for settlers and medically for the region. Durango attracted physicians from the start, probably because of its setting and they, combined with the hospital, gave Durango another advantage over its rivals. While modern medicine would not appear until World War II, Mercy Hospital still provided the best available. Over the years, the building was enlarged and treatment improved.

No major epidemics hit Durango until the flu arrived in 1918 as it did throughout the world. There existed no cure for it and millions of people died including nearly 1/10 of Silverton's population. Durango was not hit that seriously, but school, public meetings, and church services closed. Train passengers were quarantined, and people wore masks in public. Some people now regretted Colorado had gone dry back in 1916 because a good shot of liquor had once been the home cure for many aliments.

Eventually the flu threat declined and times returned to normal. Those who lived through these days never forgot the trauma. Colorado lost more than 7,000 people in three months. Interestingly, the Spanish Flu pandemic hit younger people harder than the elderly and proved especially deadly at higher elevations.

Not all people wanted to go to a Catholic Hospital with all those religious paintings and plaster saints around the halls. Nor did some ardent Protestants enjoy being treated by Catholic nuns. As a result, Durango has always had private hospitals, and later, in its existence, a community hospital. This only increased the medical opportunities available. One of the most prominent private hospitals was owned by photographer and doctor Benjamin Oschner who operated his hospital for nearly four decades into the 1930s. A brilliant surgeon, he could also be contrary and hardly a Durangoan from his era did not have a story about him.

Durango never had one of those nineteenth-century cure-all sanitariums to conquer tuberculosis, or as the victims were sometimes called, "the one lunged army." Durango did have a sanitarium, however, which promised to cure tobacco, drug, and drinking addictions with the "gold treatment." Located in west Durango near Junction Creek, it was part of a franchise operation that could be found elsewhere in the country. How successful its secret method proved may be doubted.

Durangoans prided themselves, however, on being a community of "churches and homes." The Durango Trust, the land company for the railroad, laid out Durango with a plan in mind. The noise, dust, and bustle of the business community would be along Main Avenue. Second Avenue would serve as a buffer and Third Avenue, or as it originally was named "the Boulevard," would be "the church and residential" avenue. Here folks would have a good view of the mountains, fresh air, and the quiet of a Victorian nineteenth century neighborhood. Their descendants would call this "quality of life."

The Boulevard became what its planners hoped. Those mainline Protestant churches — Methodist, Episcopal, Presbyterian, and Baptist, by the century's turn had established themselves there. The first high school also graced the street as did some of the fanciest homes in town. Then the Ladies Literary Society helped plant the trees on the parkway down the middle of the street. Once those trees grew, they

The original Mercy Hospital in Durango operated by the Sisters of Mercy.

The private Ochsner Hospital ran for four decades and was owned by a surgeon and award-winning photographer.

Third Avenue, Durango, Colo.

Early view of Third Avenue in Durango. In the newly formed town, this avenue was to be the main residential area. Today, Third Avenue is a National Historic District with many fine homes that date back to Durango's early history.

Durango Public Library, Durango, Colorado

A view of the new library built in 1907 on Second Avenue. This fine library was a result of the generosity of the multimillionaire Andrew Carnegie, who helped communities across the nation build libraries. Although slightly altered, the building is still in use today as Durango's Public Library.

provided a tree-lined avenue just like the ones residents had left at their old homes elsewhere in the country.

Durango's society lived along the street and on quiet evenings they sat on their front porches and discussed their world in the Animas Valley. Nary a Catholic church was found there, though. St. Columba set north across the river and Sacred Heart in the south end of town. The latter served a congregation mostly composed of immigrants and Hispanics who worked in the smelter and coal mines. St. Columba, on the other hand, found its membership made up mostly of northern Europeans.

That reflected somewhat the population distribution of Durango during its first few generations of residents. Northern European and American people predominated. A few Blacks and Chinese added a bit of mixture and flavor and not until 1900 would the Hispanics start arriving in larger numbers. While there would be incidents of racism, youthful fights, and tacit segregation in the south part of town for newly arrived immigrants and Hispanics, Durangoans generally got along fine with each other.

The only flare up came with the arrival of the Ku Klux Klan in the 1920s. It gained a toehold here as it did throughout the state and nation. Klan members paraded, burned crosses on Smelter Mountain, conducted Klan funerals, and gathered for social events. It disappeared nearly as fast as it came and by the end of the decade existed as only a fading memory, a memory many of its one-time members hoped to forget.

Durangoans' quality of life was also enhanced when the town built a library, but they did not do it alone. Multimillionaire, steel magnate, Andrew Carnegie believed in the idea of the "gospel of wealth." That is sharing your wealth, and he decided to do this by building libraries in communities. Silverton and Durango both benefited from his generosity.

A site was selected on Second Avenue and construction started. The library opened in 1907, another sign of Durango coming of age. Eventually they built a new high school just across the street which made it that much easier for the students. Whether or not they appreciated the advantage, Durangoans as a whole did.

The modern age came quickly to Durango. Electricity and electric lights arrived in the late 1880s and telephones were not far behind. Automobiles chugged in after the turn-of-the-century, along with the phonograph, and motion pictures. Probably the students enjoyed these new inventions more than their library or up-to-date school system.

Everything was up-to-date in Durango and no more so than when the aeroplane (as they used to call it) arrived. Not flying, as one might imagine, but boxed sitting on a flatcar. In 1903, the Wright brothers had managed to fly an aircraft. The adventure of flight had quickly caught the attention of Americans and now a decade later Durangoans were about to see a plane soaring over their town.

The aeroplane was assembled and the track around the fairgrounds used as a runway. When it took off, it set an altitude record for the time. Most Durangoans probably never expected to witness this wonder of the modern age flying over their community. School kids and adults came out to see it. They also saw one of the problems when a down draft forced it to make a crash landing on its third flight.

That was not the only problem Durango faced in those years. Back in 1911, the flood of the "century" washed out almost all the bridges from Silverton to Durango and on other rivers in southwestern Colorado. From three to five feet of water covered much of the upper Animas Valley north of town.

In Durango, the flood damaged some homes and debris piled up around the riverbanks. Other floods would follow, but none has equaled the 1911 flood. Mother Nature, however, lurks right around the corner and some day another "flood of the century" will show puny man who is the real boss.

Durango, like the rest of the country, sank into depression following the stock market crash of 1929. Locally the big blow came with the closing of the smelter in November 1930. Jobs disappeared, people lost their homes and farmers their farms, and despair settled gloomily over the city, county, country and beyond that to the world. A "Hooverville," nicknamed for the beleaguered president, sprang up between Durango and Animas City. People lived in whatever they could throw together for shelter and unfortunately, here as elsewhere, relief agencies quickly became overwhelmed.

A new era appeared in 1933 when Democratic President Franklin Roosevelt entered the White House and launched the New Deal. Never had Uncle Sam played such a role in people's lives and Americans saw the government everywhere. The New Deal touched Durango in a variety of ways. The government established a Civilian Conservation Corps camp on the mesa where the college now stands. Young men from there worked on the fairgrounds, built the Lion's Den north of the golf course, and busied themselves in a variety of jobs about town and taking courses if they had not finished high school.

The three "R's" of the New Deal — relief, recovery, and reform — kept it going throughout the decade. One of the major local projects was the construction of Vallecito Dam east of town in the valley of the Los Pinos River. When completed it provided water storage, irrigation, and a tourist attraction. After World War II, as part of the Upper Colorado River Storage Project, Lemon Dam provided the same benefits, finally providing agriculture, residents, and the Utes long-needed water.

In 1913, Durangoans were introduced to the aeroplane, which arrived by train. The aeroplane was assembled at the fairgrounds and its track served as the aeroplane's runway. At the time the plane lifted off, it set an altitude record for flying, in part because Durango's elevation is 6,500 feet.

The 1911 flood battered and destroyed bridges throughout the San Juan Basin. The Denver & Rio Grande bridge over the Animas River in Durango has fully loaded railcars situated on it to try and prevent it from washing away. They succeeded.

Construction of the Vallecito Dam east of Durango in 1939. The project was part of President Franklin Roosevelt's depression era New Deal program. The reservoir provided water storage, irrigation, and a large lake for tourist and recreation opportunities.

With the decline in gold and silver mining in the San Juan Mountains, the smelter found new life as a uranium mill. The complex processed uranium that would be used in atomic bombs and it continued this role to support the Cold War until its shutdown in 1964.

World War II brought the country out of the depression and entered the United States into a new epoch. Durangoans went to war in a variety of ways from joining the military to moving to work in defense plants, and planting victory gardens and buying war bonds at home. Across the river, at the old smelter, however, history was being made in another way. Durangoans helped create the atomic bomb.

The closed smelter was converted into a uranium mill where carnotite and pitchblende ores were refined and shipped elsewhere to produce atomic bombs. Three stood ready by the summer of 1945, one used as a test, the other two dropped on Japan to end the war. The plant shut down temporarily that year, but restarted as the Cold War against communism turned hot. Until dismantled in 1964, the plant continued operating leaving behind a "hot" tailings pile. The souvenir of yesterday was cleaned up in the 1980s.

More important for the long range history of Durango, Fort Lewis College moved into town in 1956. The old military post on the La Plata River had been converted into an Indian boarding school in 1891, then evolved through a rural high school to become a junior college in 1933. After the war, luring students to the rural setting proved hard, with only a couple hundred by the 1950s, and to save the school a change had to be made.

As a result it moved into Durango and in 1964 became a four-year liberal arts college. Over the years since, Fort Lewis has grown and, without question, advantageously possesses one of the most beautiful college locations in the country. By the opening of the twenty-first century, 4,500 students were studying there in a variety of majors.

Durango now had become a major tourist destination. Back in the 1960s, Purgatory ski area had opened north of town giving the community something it had long needed, a year around attraction to join the summer fun.

Interest in history, and Durango was steeped in it, led to a preservation movement and two historic districts — Main and Third Avenues. History sold, as well, as visitors came to appreciate the community's western heritage. The great historic attraction was the narrow gauge railroad. Along with other railroads, both passenger and freight traffic had declined over the Denver & Rio Grande lines. There was talk of abandoning the line between Durango and Silverton, but locals saved it. The trip northward through the beautiful Animas valley and canyon offered classic railroading at its best. Initially the D&RG did not see it that way, but eventually realized the tourist potential. The line survived a 1970 flood which tore out several miles of track. Repaired, the D&RG eventually sold the line, which as the Durango & Silverton Narrow Gauge Railroad continues to operate and draw rail fans and others to a "trip through yesteryear."

Thus as Durango enters into the twenty-first century, it carries with it a fascinat-

Aerial view of Fort Lewis Agricultural College along the La Plata River west of Durango. Fort Lewis began as a military post at this spot and then converted to an Indian boarding school in 1891. It evolved into a rural high school and eventually a junior college by 1933. In 1956 the college moved onto a mesa overlooking Durango and became a four-year liberal arts school in 1964. Today, the historic site is used as an agricultural station run by Colorado State University.

A Durango & Silverton Narrow Gauge Railroad engine crosses a bridge over the Animas River on its trip from Durango to Silverton. As freight and passengers declined on the Denver & Rio Grande Railroad, there was talk of abandoning the line. Citizens from Durango and Silverton refused to let that happen and were able to save the railroad for future train enthusiasts and tourists to enjoy.

ing heritage toward an exciting future. What that future might be we cannot tell, but of the past we can remember and retell.

The words of the immortal Robert Burns, Scotland's greatest poet and arguably greatest hero, captured those yesteryears. He wrote, in his lowland Scottish dialect, one of his most famous poems, "Auld Lang Syne."

Should auld acquaintance be foregot,
And never brought to mind?
Should auld acquantance be forgot,
And auld lang syne!

For auld lang syne, my dear,
For auld lang syne,
We'll tak a cup o' kindness yet
For auld lang syne! ◆

Main Avenue of Durango decked out to welcome visitors to its historic downtown in this postcard postmarked 1953.

Drilling a hole thousands of feet underground at the Silver Lake Mine near Silverton, Colorado. The ruins of the Silver Lake Mine are still visible today, with many artifacts from this operation strewn about the ground.

Far right: Four men riding the tram system at the Sunnyside Mine near Silverton, Colorado. The aerial trams were an efficient way to move ore, supplies and men between the mill and the mine.

Drilling Hole 3,000 ft. under ground. Silver Lake Mine. Silverton, Colo.

24. SILVERTON, COLORADO.   COPYRIGHT, 1901, BY DETROIT PHOTOGRAPHIC CO.

Early view of Silverton, Colorado looking south. The magnificent town hall and grand county courthouse have yet to be built.

Rapid Transit, Sunnyside Mine, Silverton, Colo.

SILVERTON

———⊶✦⊷———

In the spring of 1874, word filtered out that the newest settlement
in Baker's Park had a name: Quito, named after the capitol of Ecuador,
which was also 9,300 feet above sea level. Some folks didn't care for that name
and two names were proposed: Greenville and Silverton. Silverton won.
It is likely that the names proponents simply applied the precious metals name
to the traditional contraction for "town" and came up with Silverton.

— from *Many More Mountains, Vol. 1* – Allen Nossaman

SILVERTON THROUGH THE YEARS

BY BEV RICH AND FREDA PETERSON

Although life and the environment in Silverton have always been a bit more severe than in most locations, what with howling blizzards and avalanches, the hardships were balanced by fun-loving and happy times. The Niegold brothers, Reinhardt and Gustave, and their half-brother, Oscar Roedel, came to the Silverton area in the 1870s. They had acquired the cultivated tastes of their German ancestors, and were noted for their lavish style of living and entertaining. Their standard of living included the best in food and drink — imported wines and Turkish tobacco. Their gourmet meals were prepared from German, Russian and Italian cookbooks. Musically inclined, Reinhardt was an accomplished pianist, and Gus had been a professional opera singer in New York City. They entertained their friends by performing in Knickerbocker pants, powdered hair and buckle shoes.

For Marie Hollingsworth, one of her happiest moments was her very first meal in Silverton. She and her sister, Emma, came over the plains and mountains from Missouri in 1878. Their father and brothers had settled in Silverton earlier and arranged for the sisters to join them after their education was completed.

The girls rode the train to Fort Garland, Colorado, the end of the line. From there to Del Norte they traveled by horse-drawn wagon, then on to Lost Trail. At Grassy Hill, the western side of Stony Pass and the Continental Divide, the night was spent under heaven's canopy, with a bag of shelled corn for a pillow. Early the next morning the party started over the rugged range, then down into Cunningham Gulch, which was one huge melting snowslide strewn with boulders and giant spruce trees splintered into kindling wood by the force of the snow. That weary night was spent at Howardsville, and the next morning they continued walking toward Silverton. When they arrived, a sumptuous noon repast awaited them. For the rest of her life, Marie Hollingsworth remembered that meal as absolutely the very best of her lifetime. It consisted of roast beef, chow-chow (a relish), canned corn, canned tomatoes and coffee.

Sixteen years later Silverton had progressed. In the spring and summer of 1894, the Miners Band decided to build a bandstand on Greene Street between 12th and 13th, in the middle of the street. Built around a pole, the stand itself was 12 feet off the ground. When completed, the Miners Band gave a grand open air concert in its new bandstand, concluding with the Star Spangled Banner. Evidently, the bandstand

SILVERTON, COLORADO (ALT. 9288 FT.) AND ANIMAS RIVER

Silverton sits at an elevation close to 9,300 feet. Notice the train tracks in the foreground and the Animas River to their right. The Denver & Rio Grande Railroad entered town in 1882.

The Contention Mill Boarding House for miners near Silverton. Only a handful of boarding houses still stand intact around the San Juan Mountains.

Ready for the Mines, Silverton, Colo.

Pack animals are loaded with supplies for their trip to the mines near Silverton. On their return trip they will pack down ore from the mines. Before good roads and ore wagons, aerial trams, and the railroad, pack animals were one of the only forms of transportation to haul ore from the mines.

Silverton & Kendell Mts., Silverton, Colo.

View of Silverton, Colorado with Kendall Mountain to the east. This postcard was sent in 1911 to wish someone a happy birthday.

was less than a success with either the band or the citizens, and was ridiculed in the newspaper as "an eyesore to the Silverton people." It was referred to as a "buzzards roost which should be removed," and three years after it was built, it was removed. It was hoped it could be used as a judges' stand at a racetrack in the future.

The birthday of Bobby Burns, Scotland's poet who died at the age of 29, was observed in Silverton with a yearly Bobby Burns Celebration. In 1897, Burns' 138th birthday, the event was remembered by speech, music, song, dance and feast at the courthouse under the auspices of the Caledonian Club. The newspaper reported that the efforts of Scotland's sons were not in vain, and that the entertainment was one of the best "jollifications" that had occurred in Silverton. The courthouse had a capacity of 275 people, and many more had to be turned away. The music, speeches, and the dancing of the Highland Fling were enjoyed to the utmost. At 10:30 the hall was cleared of seats and the dancing commenced. It abated only at 3:30 a.m. because of the sheer exhaustion of the musicians.

Soon after the Bobby Burns affair, an impromptu dance was held at the Hotel Grand at the invitation of a few of "the boys." The verbal invitations were extended, eight or ten couples responded and danced until 1 o'clock! The music was good, the floor was smooth, and a good time was had by all.

In 1898 another popular winter event was a Masque Carnival at the skating rink, attended by 150 people. About half the guests wore a variety of costumes and ugly faces. About 15 boys and girls representing the Salvation Army marched through the streets with tambourine and drum and sang hymns to the tune of "Hot Time in the Old Town," etc., followed by a curious crowd of hoodlums. Prizes were handed out for the best costumes.

Fraternal lodges were popular in Silverton, and the Knights of Pythias held a ball at the courthouse in 1898. Invitations were issued and preparations were made for a glorious time. The hall was festive with red, white and blue banners and festoons. While dancing was in progress, luncheon was served, and those wishing to smoke cigars were invited to do so in the rooms of the county judge.

Silverton is known for its great Fourth of July celebrations. In 1901, the day was filled with a parade, drilling contests, a baseball game, a five-mile cowboy relay race in which each "cowboy" changed horses each mile, an inspiring speech by Congressman John C. Bell, fireworks and that evening a Woodmen of the World ball. The celebration spilled over to the next day when there was a 100-yard foot race for boys under eighteen, another 100-yard race for men, a bicycle race, a contest of climbing the greased pole, and another to catch a greased pig.

Two months later, on Labor Day, there was baseball, a nine-mile bicycle race, more baseball games and a fifteen-round boxing glove contest at the opera house. This was followed by a big dance and "it was not until the wee sma' hours that the merry crowd wended their way homeward."

A wedding in a mine boarding house? This took place in January of 1907. Ike Camp was head tram man at the Grand Mogul Mine near Gladstone. He was one of the best known tramway men in Colorado, and was an expert on the mines and mills of the San Juan. His advice was ever sought in matters of tramlines, cable ways and transportation of ores. He and the schoolteacher at Gladstone, Carrie Frances Sweezy, fell in love and decided to marry. The wedding was novel and unique, held in the mine boarding house. The dining room had been decorated with flags and festoons, and at 9:00 p.m. the bride and groom entered the room. The Rev. C.A. Mohr of Silverton performed the ceremony before the 46 guests, after which all were served a wedding supper which included everything good and tempting.

In 1908 the Miners Union gave a grand masque ball at its hall on New Year's Eve. The boys intended to make it an unparalleled social event in the history of Silverton. Costumes were available at Dan Sheahans's and were to be "strictly up-to-date!" Tickets were the usual price for gentleman and lady, with an extra charge of 25 cents for children and extra ladies.

This 1909 postcard shows 10 feet of snow piled along the streets of Silverton. Locals call this a typical winter.

Clearing a snowslide from the Denver & Rio Grande Railroad tracks leading into Silverton. The workers are trying to clear the tracks with hand shovels. Unemployed miners welcomed blizzards because they earned a days wage clearing snow off railroad tracks.

View of Silverton's Greene Street, the main thoroughfare ca. 1950s. Many mining towns do not exist any more or have few historic structures because major fires destroyed them. Silverton's historic downtown buildings have survived because there has never been a major fire.

91381 ARASTRA GULCH, SILVERTON, COLO.

Old Way of Transportation. Silverton. Colo.

Top right: The Ross Smelter sat at the north end of Silverton while another smelter, the Walsh Smelter, was situated at the south end of town. The smelting industry was short lived in Silverton as the town of Durango soon took over and became a regional smelting center.

Right: Early view of Arrastra Gulch near Silverton. This is where some of the earliest and most successful mines were worked. Notice the water flume in the foreground, which was torn down in the late 1920s or early 1930s.

Right: "Old Way of Transportation." Pack animals are loaded with timbers bound for a mine near Silverton. This form of transportation was being made obsolete with the rise of aerial tramways. Only the most remote mines, without access to roads or trams, continued to use pack animals. This put them at an economic disadvantage.

The Hamlet Mill near Silverton during the early 1900s in this color postcard. Many of the mining structures around Silverton have disappeared due to salvage of their timber, the ravages of time or vandalism. All that is left to indicate a structure had been there may be a foundation.

Hamlet Mill, near Silverton, Colo.

91379 SILVERTON-RED MOUNTAIN WAGON ROAD

An ore wagon makes its way down the Silverton - Red Mountain Wagon Road. This road, eventually stretching between Silverton and Ouray, became known as the Million Dollar Highway in the 1920s and continues to draw many tourists today to its scenic vistas, tight turns, and steep canyons.

Far left: The present school building was built in 1911 when it housed the High School. This was at a time when Silverton had a much larger population. Today, the building houses grades K - 12 and at times has only a handful of students due to a smaller population of families with children.

91370 HIGH SCHOOL, SILVERTON, COLO.

Early 1900s postcard of Silverton's Public Library. The building was constructed in 1906 and was a Carnegie-funded library. Today, the library looks much the same on the exterior and interior.

The Western Federation of Miners completed the Miners Union Hall in 1901 and it became the home of a number of labor organizations in the community. The second floor contained a large dance floor for social occasions.

On the other side of Greene Street, prostitutes were numerous in Silverton's early years. In 1885 it was estimated about 130 were making a living on Blair Street; in 1929 there were still 32 in town. Some of their colorful nicknames were Broken Nose Grace, Dago Tina, Dutch Lena, Irish Nellie, Jew Fanny, Minnie the Baby Jumbo, Old Gray Mare, Nigger Lola, Unregenerative Mary, White Nigger, Big Billie, Denver Kate, 21 Pearl, Blonde Peggy, Oregon Short Line, Sheeny Pearl, Black Minnie, Tar Baby, Big Tillie and Crazy Horse. Jew Fanny was one of the last to leave town; she observed that she couldn't make a living at prostitution when so many other women were "giving it away."

The 1900 census reported a little over 2,300 people in the county, and in 1901 there were 137 telephones in Silverton. The decade of 1900 to 1910 saw a burst of building activity along Silverton's Greene Street, the main street of town (named for one of the pioneers). Concrete sidewalks became a reality, and a municipally owned light plant provided electricity to the booming town. A modern water system and sewer lines were installed, greatly improving living conditions. The Carnegie Library, courthouse, town hall, Wyman and Benson buildings, Miners Union Hall and Miners Union Hospital were built in that glittering decade; all were substantial structures and are still standing and in use. The 1910 county population was a little over 3,000 people, and then began to decline.

A SILVERTON "FALLEN ANGEL" OBSERVED "…THAT SHE COULDN'T MAKE A LIVING AT PROSTITUTION WHEN SO MANY OTHER WOMEN WERE 'GIVING IT AWAY'."

Several boom and bust cycles typical of mining towns ensued. Silverton survived, but the other mining camps in the county became ghostly reminders of the past. However, during the Great Depression, Silverton became one of the few mining towns in actual operation in the West. Led by Charles A. Chase, a syndicate bankrolled in Kansas City was formed to buy up old workings in Arrastra Gulch — the Shenandoah-Dives group. In 1929, he built the Mayflower Mill, now a National Historic Landmark, to process the ore. The Mayflower Mill was the last major accomplishment of Chase, a metallurgist and successful mining man. Chase gambled that base metals — lead, copper and zinc — could carry the costs of operation, with a little profit coming from gold and silver. His gamble paid off and miners worked until 1939 when a bitter strike ensued. Although holding out for a time, eventually the union was broken, and the mine and mill were worked by non-union workers until 1952.

During World War II, base metals were considered strategic metals and mining was considered strategic labor. The Idarado Mine linked the Treasury Tunnel on the Red Mountain side with old workings at Telluride to mine for the war effort. For years it ranked first or second in the state in the production of copper, lead, zinc, cadmium, silver and gold.

In 1959, Standard Uranium Company bought the Sunnyside Mine, which had been closed since the mid-1930s. Miners drove the American Tunnel from Gladstone under the old workings and proceeded to mine the grand old mine for the next 19 years, until the unimaginable happened: Lake Emma collapsed through the mine. In its 130-year-history, miners at the Sunnyside had driven over 80 miles of tunnels inside the mountain, which was topped by Lake Emma. There were rich gold veins close to the bottom of the lake and miners were instructed to drive drift towards them. As the tunnel drove closer to the bottom of the Lake, warm air rose and melted hoarfrost in fractures under the lake. On June 4, 1978 — a Sunday — the bottom of Lake Emma gave out and millions of gallons of water poured through the mine, gushing out of the portal at Gladstone, carrying mine timber, ore cars and debris for a hundred miles south. Thankfully, no one was killed because the miners didn't work on Sunday. After repairing the damage, the Sunnyside opened again and ran under successive owners until 1991. Modern environmental practices and global economics closed the last mine in San Juan County, changing its history forever. Like the Sunnyside, the famous Idarado Mine also closed and began to implement a multi-million dollar reclamation plan.

Summer Scene at Iowa and Silver Lake Mine, Altitude 12000 feet, near Silverton, Colo.

91384 SILVER LAKE MILL & NEAR SILVE

Top: The Silver Lake Mine complex that sat at 12,000 feet dwarfs two men in a boat on Silver Lake. The ruins of the Silver Lake and Iowa mines are still visible with many artifacts half-buried in the sand.

Near right: Early 1900s postcard of the large Silver Lake Mill that was located near the Animas River and the tracks of the Silverton Northern Railroad. The mill was connected to the Silver Lake Mine at 12,000 feet by an aerial tram system that moved ore from the mine to the mill in large buckets. The Aspen Mine is in the background.

Far right: The Gold King Mill was located in the Cement Creek drainage near Gladstone, just north of Silverton.

HEAD-ON OF THE "SILVER VISTA" ARRIVING IN SILVERTON JUNE 22, 1947

Sanborn X-1250

The "Silver Vista" train arriving in Silverton, 1947. Mining was still the major economic industry for Silverton, but tourism was gaining in economic importance.

The "Painted Train" making its way between Silverton and Durango.

FIRST TRIP "PAINTED TRAIN" NARROW GAUGE, SILVERTON, COLORADO 9300 FT.

The Denver & Rio Grande Railroad arrived in Silverton in 1882. It carried ore to the smelter in Durango and freight up into the mountains to Silverton and the high mountain camps. After the closure of the Mayflower Mine in 1952, there was no ore to carry and the railroad tried to abandon the line. With the emergence of the modern automobile after World War II, train usage declined and thousands of miles of track had been abandoned in Colorado. City fathers in Durango and Silverton fought the abandonment, taking their campaign to the Public Utilities Commission in Washington, D.C. They were successful, and today 200,000 passengers a year ride the scenic route.

Although always a tourist town, Silverton saw the emergence of modern tourism in the 1950s. The "Western" movie was popular and several movies were shot in Silverton, starring some of the biggest names in Hollywood: John Wayne, Jimmy Stewart and Marilyn Monroe, among them. Another famous movie filmed with the Durango-Silverton train was the 1968 classic Western "Butch Cassidy and the Sundance Kid" starring Robert Redford and Paul Newman.

The highways into Silverton were paved, making it easier for mom, dad, and the kids to load up the Hudson or the Studebaker and make a trip to Silverton. Motor hotels sprang up and Silverton's Blair Street looked like a Hollywood set, complete with gunfights staged at noon in front of the Bent Elbow when the train arrived. These staged gunfights were historically inaccurate. Silverton always had sheep and sheepherders, who came up and

The Silverton business district looking north, ca. 1940s. The entire town of Silverton was designated a National Historic Landmark in 1962.

BUSINESS DISTRICT - SILVERTON COLO.

over the old passes, but there were never cows and cowboys or gunfights on Main Street.

The "jeep" had been invented for use as a utility vehicle during World War II. Veterans soon saw the prospect of using the rugged little vehicles for pleasure on old mine roads in the mountains and "4-wheeling" became the vogue. The ATV has made backcountry access easier than ever, and the Alpine Loop, one of the state's premier scenic drives, has become a destination for thousands of backcountry enthusiasts.

Silverton is also fun for kids. Fishing at the "Kid's Pond," an early fishery used to raise fish to stock the high country lakes, was restricted to kids under twelve years old. Silverton girls were horrified when the boys would eat worms. Another long-time tradition for children is Santa coming to town to give out sacks of candy at the Town Christmas tree, right in the middle of Greene Street, on Christmas Eve. Santa is escorted into town by Silverton's volunteer Fire Department, riding in the restored 1929 Chevy firetruck. Now a new generation is discovering Silverton's magnificent location, deep snows, stirring mountains, and congenial residents. Silverton through the decades has always been a celebration of survival and endurance, but in the 21st century this mining town has a new lease on life — as a recreation and tourist Mecca for those outdoor enthusiasts interested in rock climbing, ice climbing, and some of the deepest powder skiing in the West. A new future for an old town is an exciting prospect. ◆

Notorious Blair Street in Silverton, Colorado. It was on this street where there was a flourishing red-light district and "proper" women dared not be seen.

The Christ of the Mines Shrine stands on the slopes of Anvil Mountain overlooking the town of Silverton. The idea for the shrine developed in 1958 to help provide hope for the depressed economy in the town. The statue is sculpted from Italian Carerra marble.

Golden aspen trees shimmer in a beautiful autumn afternoon in Silverton, Colorado.

The writer of this 1923 postcard visited her brother at the Camp Bird Mine and commented on the beautiful scenery near Ouray, Colorado.

Below: Early 20th century view of Ouray, looking south towards Mount Abrams.

A 1920s view of the Camp Bird Mine and Mill near Ouray.

Travelers along the road between Ouray and Yankee Boy Basin. They are at a narrow spot known as Hanging Rock on a section or road constructed by Otto Mears around 1883.

HAND-COLORED
POST CARD

OURAY
SEP
17
5 PM
1923
COLO.

Published by The Wardell Store Co.
Mill and Tunnel, Camp Bird, Ltd., Ouray, Colo.

Post Cards of Quality.— The Albertype Co., Brooklyn, N. Y.

THIS SPACE FOR MESSAGE.

THIS SPACE FOR ADDRESS.

Ouray, Colo., Looking South

OURAY

———⊰◈◈◈⊱———

Established in 1875, the town of Ouray
was named for the well-known Ute leader, Chief Ouray
(sometimes the name was spelled "Ure").
The mining camp was first known as
Uncompahgre or Uncompahgre City.
It became the capital of Ouray County.

OURAY –
THE SWITZERLAND OF AMERICA

BY ANN HOFFMAN

Majestic mountains, some rising more than thirteen thousand feet above sea level; mesas and valleys; timberline and tundra; deep blue skies; abundant sunshine; wildflowers; forests of tall pine, spruce, fir, and aspen trees interspersed with subalpine growths of juniper, cedar, pinon, yucca, and sagebrush; streams, creeks, waterfalls, and the Uncompahgre River; reservoirs, ponds, lakes, parks; hundreds of jeep and hiking trails; wildlife, birds and fish; mines, mills and minerals; ghost towns; hot and cold springs; and ranches with cattle, horses, sheep, llamas, camels. All this describes the physical attributes of southwestern Colorado's Ouray County.

From a geological perspective, the magnificent surroundings Ouray County residents and visitors enjoy today were formed over millions of years from glaciation, water carving and volcanic activity, resulting in the most mineralized mountain range in Colorado, the San Juans. Centuries before Spanish explorers, French trappers,

Panoramic view of Ouray and Mount Abrams in the distance. Notice the railroad cars in the lower right corner. The railroad first entered Ouray in 1887 and dramatically lowered costs of incoming supplies and outgoing ore from the mines.

View of Mount Sneffels with Twin Falls in the foreground. Both can be reached by a spectacular jeep ride into Yankee Boy Basin. Wildflowers are at their best in late July and early August.

Early 20th century view of Main Street in Ouray. The grand Beaumont Hotel is at the right of the postcard.

1091-A   Beaumont Hotel, Ouray, Colorado

A stagecoach is parked in front of the magnificent Beaumont Hotel. The Beaumont opened in 1887 and immediately added a touch of elegance to the mining town of Ouray.

The writer asks the recipient of this postcard if they remember Ouray. How could one forget the rugged beauty around Ouray? The postcard was sent in December of 1922.

and various prospectors arrived, the Uncompahgre or Tabeguache Ute Indians roamed these parts during the warm months of the year, staying close to the Ouray mountain valley, the Uncompahgre River, and living in stick houses called "wickiups." These Utes were a nomadic tribe who came into their revered San Juan Mountains to hunt, soak in the hot springs to cleanse and heal themselves, and for ceremonial purposes. Among the ceremonies was the offering of gifts to the waters to appease the mythical "water babies." The Utes had an ancient spiritual relationship with the copious hot springs in Ouray County. Chief Ouray's mother was a Tabeguache Ute; thus Ouray spent much time amidst her people in this land, learning much from them. It is said that, as an adult, Chief Ouray built a summer house at a hot springs in the vicinity of the current city of Ouray. An archaeological assessment is being conducted that may prove this theory.

For more than a century picturesque Ouray County has been a destination for travelers and settlers alike. It is an awesome landmass with steep gorges, rugged towering peaks, tumbling waterfalls, high mesas and green pastures. Three charming municipalities as well as many "ghost" towns/camps beckon visitors from around the world. Ouray, a jewel-like Victorian city, is a registered National Historic District nestled in a high mountain valley into which flow waterfalls and streams. The city's earliest inhabitants were miners, merchants, freighters, bankers, teachers, ministers, newspaper publishers, and their families. Ridgway, a ranching town to the north of

Early 1920s hand-colored postcard of the Sneffels Road between Ouray and Yankee Boy Basin. Notice the remnants of a snowslide still in the creek during the summer.

Ouray, spreads itself out across open terrain on both sides of the Uncompahgre River, and is ringed by ranches and horse farms. Both Ridgway and Ouray espoused the railroad; Ridgway formerly being a railroad hub and home to many railroaders. Ridgway was also the home of the seven famous "Galloping Geese." They were all built here. What were the galloping geese? Surprisingly enough they were half-car or bus and half-railroad car. They were used in the last days of the narrow gauge railroad to economically deliver mail and supplies and to haul workers. These novel conveyances did in fact waddle down the railroad tracks, which is how they got their name. You can see a replica of Goose #1 at Ridgway today. It even runs on a short stretch of track at the Ridgway Fairgrounds.

Citizens work to clean up mud and debris from a large flood in Ouray. In 1911, the San Juan Mountains experienced massive floods that destroyed homes, property, and downtowns throughout many communities.

"THE CITY BECAME A UNIQUE MINING TOWN FILLED WITH EAGER MEN AND FORMIDABLE WOMEN SEEKING A QUICK FORTUNE AS WELL AS THOSE WHO WERE DETERMINED TO TURN FAST FORTUNES INTO A FINE VICTORIAN CITY ESPOUSING MANY AMENITIES AND CULTURAL ADVANTAGES FOR THEMSELVES AND THEIR FAMILIES."

A close up view of the workings at Camp Bird Mine near Ouray. Discovered by Tom Walsh, Camp Bird Mine produced millions of dollars worth of gold between 1896 and 1910 and became known as one of the richest mines in the world. The boarding house still stands.

Tiny Colona, at the north end of Ouray County, was a farming and ranching community (and still is); a supply point and an old stage stop in the early days. Today, the town is home to the oldest church in the county (the 1878 church was razed in Ouray and moved by wagon to Colona in 1912 where it was reconstructed.). Church services are still held in that building on Sundays.

To the south, Highway 550 (aka "The Million Dollar Highway" and "The San Juan Skyway") winds its way over breathtaking narrow cliff-hanging roads as it climbs over the magnificent Red Mountain Pass, descending then into Silverton. Westward from Ridgway, Highway 62 crosses the Dallas Divide, along the old narrow gauge railroad grade past the frequently photographed Sneffels Range, on its way to Telluride.

Ouray, known as the "gem of the Rockies," was first settled in 1875 when a few hardy miners crossed the mountains from Howardsville, near Silverton, and discov-

Camp Bird Mine. Ouray, Colo.

Circle Route Stage 20, Ouray, Colo.

Left: Circle Route Stage 20 ready to begin a trip on the rough roads that lead out of Ouray. Early transportation routes from the mining towns were long, bumpy and difficult.

Below: This 1905 postcard shows a burro pack train on the trail to the Army and Navy Mine near Ouray. Notice how the timbers are lashed to the burros and just imagine the weight of this cargo.

Looking out from the dark interior of Box Canyon in Ouray.

No. 1. Burro Pack Train, En Route to the Army and Navy Mine, Ouray, Colorado.
Published by The Ouray Drug Company, Ouray, Colorado.

Cascade Falls, Ouray, Colorado

Far left: Early 1900s view of stunning Cascade Falls just east of Ouray.

Tourists on a jeep ride appear to be on the verge of a dark abyss along the Camp Bird Road into Yankee Boy Basin. This high point overlooks the site of Camp Bird Mine.

ered silver, gold, and other precious ores in the area. That first winter, there were thirteen men who lived at the Ouray town site, which at that time was nothing but a tiny mining camp called Uncompahgre, the Ute word for warm, flowing water. Some say the first dwelling at the Ouray town site was an old New Mexico style adobe dwelling thought to be the summer hunting lodge of Chief Ouray. Others say the first building was, and still is, the little cabin on the east hillside of Ouray near Portland Creek at Fifth Street and Fourth Avenue along what is now an alley. And yet, others think the first home, a cabin, was that of Gus Begole in the Mineral Farm area.

In 1875 word spread quickly about the discovery of silver and gold at the foot of Mount Hayden in the vicinity of the little mining camp called Uncompahgre. It spread across the mountains and even around the world. In 1876, Uncompahgre became the patented and incorporated city of Ouray, thanks to Captain Milton Cline and others. The city became a unique mining town filled with eager men and formidable women seeking a quick fortune as well as those who were determined to turn fast fortunes into a fine Victorian city espousing many amenities and cultural advantages for themselves and their families. The city soon had its own waterworks, electricity, fire protection (the Ouray Hose Company), a community hall, three churches, and an organized school district. By 1881, Edward Wright, one of the first settlers in Ouray, had built his, still standing, substantial two-story frame building at the corner of Fifth Avenue and Main Street. Between 1886 and 1888, St. Joseph's Miners Hospital, the County Courthouse, the Beaumont Hotel, and the Wright Opera House were built. The "red-light" district was con-

Vistaland Art Ce[nter]
OURAY, COLORADO

A bright coat of pink paint covered the once grand Beaumont Hotel in the 1950s. The Beaumont sat empty for 34 years before it was purchased in 1998 and during the ensuing six years its owners have been meticulously restoring the Beaumont to its original grandeur.

Early view of the Grammar School in Ouray.

EAR CREEK FALLS NEAR OURAY, COLO.

Bear Creek Falls has a beautiful and steep drop into the Uncompahgre Gorge. It is at Bear Creek Falls that Otto Mears constructed his tollbooth for his toll road between Ouray and Red Mountain. Many miners and travelers tried to follow another trail over the mountains to avoid paying the "excessive" toll.

tained to the west of Main Street between Eighth and Tenth avenues. By 1897 the civic-minded Ouray Woman's Club was in full swing, its motto being self improvement and community service. They advertised themselves as a service club, not a social club; however, they went on the record saying: "Fear not, we do socialize even though we work." Their membership consisted of the most outstanding women in the community, all married to men who were community leaders.

Prior to the "Silver Crisis" of 1893, Ouray had grown in size to become a city of more than 2,500 citizens, perhaps even 3,000. Today, population changes significantly throughout the year. In summer the population may swell to close to 1,000. Wintertime often sees a reduction to 800 or less.

While some things change very little, like the Amphitheater, Mount Abram and Mount Hayden, Cascade Falls and Box Canyon Falls; other things change much. There are no more freight wagons, stagecoaches, pack trains, duels on Main Street, narrow gauge trains, toll roads, alligators in the hot springs pool, blacksmith shops, or assay offices. Today, while Ouray maintains much of its early Victorian flavor, it no longer is a bustling mining city. Ouray now has quiet winters interspersed with dog sledding, Nordic skiing, and ice climbing events. In summer the city is filled with tourists visiting our many shops and galleries, strolling through the streets, hiking in the hills, soaking up the beauty that surrounds them, bathing in the hot springs, and learning bits and pieces about our colorful history. Come see for yourself. ◆

Jeep trip stopped at Oh! Point near Engineer Mountain east of Ouray. That says it all!

Elk in front of Ouray Lodge No. 492 B. P. O. Elks. Are they waiting for the next meeting to start?

Early 1900s view of the pool at the Ouray Hot Springs. The shape of the pool and the facilities have changed over the years, but tourists still enjoy the soothing, hot water of the springs.

Far right: The town of Telluride sits in a box canyon and this early 1900s view is looking down Main Street toward the head of the canyon.

Mules hauled mail to the mines all year round. High elevation and deep snow were no exceptions. Miners wanted to have mail and news from the outside world, and several loyal mailmen died in avalanches.

mail coming on pack mules to a camp mine

10,000 feet above sea level

MAIN STREET, TELLURIDE, COLO.

A jeep makes its way down the treacherous Black Bear Pass Road. Telluride and the sandy-looking tailings ponds of mining operations sit in the valley below.

TELLURIDE

Incorporated as "Columbia" on July 13, 1878,
the principal mining camp on the San Miguel River
changed its name to "Telluride" at the request of U.S. Post
Office officials. A town in California called Columbia was
causing confusion among postal employees who failed to
notice the difference bewtween "California" and "Colorado."
The new named derived from tellurium ore, said to be found
in the district. Railroad conductors drew this out to the now
famous, "To-hell-you-ride." After San Miguel County was
created from the western portion of Ouray County,
Telluride became the new county's seat.

Mining the Gold:
Telluride and San Juan History

By Art Goodtimes

In Telluride, it was always about the gold. For the Utes, the golden-leaved aspen trees made the San Juans part of their "Shining Mountains," and for them San Miguel Park where Telluride now thrives was a wild box canyon of bear, trout and eagles. A good place to hunt, if not to live. Spectacular country, boasting two stunning waterfalls and a cirque of Fourteeners, but forbidding in the long winter, with mudslides, cloudbursts, avalanches, and rocky terrain.

For the Spanish, gold was the Cibola they sought everywhere in the New World. And in the San Juans they looked for it, but didn't find much. Arrastras (from Spanish for a "stone mill," used in Territorial New Mexico by gold seekers for "a mortar and pestle method of crushing ore") were the first technology to mar the alpine landscape of the region, with slave traders from Santa Fe doing most of the exploring about the high peaks and steep canyons. They found some color in the streams, but never enough to make anyone rich.

For the Anglo fur trappers, beaver was the gold they found in abundance — pelts worth a pretty penny on the East Coast drew them deep into the West's interior. Constantly on the move, they'd lay their traplines, harvest out the plentiful beaver, skin the hides, and haul them back to the trading posts. Hard, lonely work. But the profits could be formidable.

For the American settlers, it, too, was precious metal that brought them into the mountains that the new nation had avoided on its first pass across the landscape. The Rockies were too forbidding for the first pioneers, intent on the easy land pickings to be found in California or Oregon. But rumors of silver and gold brought one rush, and then another. And soon, in spite of treaties, few trails, and inhospitable conditions, the prospectors found their way into isolated San Miguel Park.

Finally, long after the mining era had passed and Telluride had devolved into a skeleton of its mining camp heyday, snow was the white gold that drew urban refugees to rumors of a new ski area about to launch. Jackson Hole, Aspen and Vail were all successful resorts, and Telluride was poised to take off for anyone willing to get in on the ground floor. That was back in the 1970s, and thirty years later Telluride now ranks with some of the most popular ski resorts in North America.

I was one of those last wave refugees from the urban madness of California.

Bird's-eye-view of Telluride, Colorado. Trails lead up the mountainsides to various mines in the region.

Snowmelt from the mountains swells the creeks that feed Bridal Veil and Ingraham Falls near Telluride. Visitors in the foreground enjoy the views of these roaring falls during a beautiful early summer day.

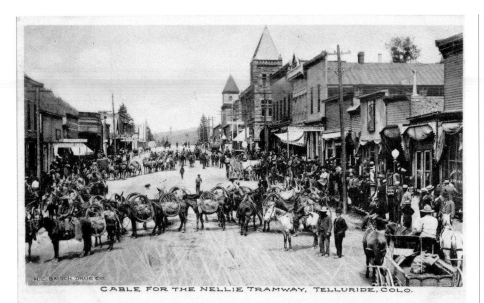

CABLE FOR THE NELLIE TRAMWAY, TELLURIDE, COLO.

People gather in downtown Telluride to see the cable that will support the tramway for the Nellie Mine. Pack animals have the heavy wire cable strapped to their sides for the trip to the mine.

Wintry scene of 1930s downtown Telluride. Visitors can still stay at the historic Sheridan Hotel and enjoy the view of the high peaks that surround the town.

Greetings From Telluride, Colo.

Looking for beauty and a good place to work and raise children. I woke up one morning after hitchhiking into Telluride to visit friends, took one look at the ivory-mantled high peaks, and I was snared. Colorado had me in its golden grip.

Give me the trembling aspens on Coonskin Hill any day, with their litter of gold and fractured sunlight. The fields of dandelions that cover the valley floor in the spring. Those rust bucket ruins in the high country above town that were once pounding mills and mines, marmots dashing now through the splayed cable and broken-down shanties. Ore heaps where I'd find quartz, crystals and maybe just a fleck of fool's gold. But even as a newcomer, I was drawn to the region's history.

✦ ✦ ✦

My mother had been a Native Daughter of the Golden West. She could trace her family back seven generations in California. Back to a Spanish *jefe de policia* in Monterey in the 1790s. And San Francisco had been our home for the last four of those generations — where I was born, my mother was born, my grandfather and my great-grandfather, whose body lies in the cemetery at the Presidio.

My dad was of immigrant stock. One generation removed from the Old Country. Italy. Naples and Abruzzi. And his ethnic family clan had moved from the Bronx to the Bay Area back in the 1920s, when he was a small child.

Telluride's history appealed to me. The story of the Italian union miners organizing a strike and battling the ruthless mine owners resonated in my own Italian blood. And the many local Spanish place names reminded me of my own Spanish roots.

One of the first things I did when I came to stay was join the local historical society board — a mostly social group of old-timers with hardly enough money in hand to keep the doors open but charged with preserving a rag tag collection of local memorabilia housed in a dilapidated stone ex-hospital building in serious danger of collapse. I was secretary, and one of my duties, besides taking notes, was cleaning the clinkers out of the coal furnace. Quickly I got in touch with the region's bygone era — hearing the stories, handling the artifacts, lifting fused vitreous matter from out of the dead embers of the antique coal hearth.

Later, taking up as a journalist, I began writing the first historical column in many a year in the pages of the upstart *San Miguel Journal*. In transforming a busted almost-ghost town into a bustling ski metropolis, local entrepreneurs had hit upon the idea of making the downtown core a National Historic Landmark District. In a few years, a Historic and Architectural Review Commission was formed, and all the mining camp Victorian buildings on the alluvial fan of tempestuous Cornet Creek were protected from inconsistent development.

Truth was, most folks who moved into Telluride in the 1970s and 1980s were from somewhere else. History may have been a selling point for the realtors and a market niche for the resort, but few of the real old-timers were left in town who cared deeply about the history of the area and worked to preserve it.

Elvira Wunderlich and Irene Visitin were among the exceptions. Happy to see the town rescued from obscurity, but wary of the new wealth and urban émigrés flooding the valley, in 1976 they began publishing a monthly newsletter about this special place they called "The Most Beautiful Spot on Earth." It was an interesting and always useful compendium of selected news, accounts of travel by–, and updates on–, former residents (part of the wider Telluride diaspora), plus the sisters' own historically-minded takes on local events. Only quite recently, after 26 years of effort, have they finally ceased monthly publication. But one would be hard-pressed to find local residents more intimately in touch with Telluride's past than Elvira and Irene.

Thus, I began a column tracking one of the local papers from a hundred years earlier — from a Save-the-Union Republican weekly called the *San Miguel Examiner*. Lots of sifting through the week's news and selecting the more interesting tidbits and unique tales from the past. Occasionally making a few of my own comments.

I learned about a tramcar that was turned into a postal conveyance, the only ore bucket post office in the nation, or so the paper from back then opined. And I followed the run-up to, the accounts of, and the aftermath relating to the Labor Struggles of 1901-04.

How Western Federation of Miners labor activist Vincent St. John bare-handedly disarmed mine owner thug Shadigee Bill on Colorado Avenue as he discharged his pistol, preventing anyone from being harmed when the tough guy tried to strong-

The writer of this 1925 postcard contemplated going to school at Stanford University in California because it provided a good education.

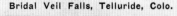

Bridal Veil Falls, Telluride, Colo.

Top right: Close-up view of Bridal Veil Falls and the powerhouse that is perched precariously at its edge. The historic powerhouse continues to sit atop the falls, but no longer provides power to the town of Telluride.

Right: Citizens work with a fire hose to try and clean up the debris and mud that has covered the streets of Telluride during the 1911 flood. During this year, devastating floods created havoc in many communities of the San Juan Mountains.

Panoramic view of the unusual rock formation known as Lizard Head. The spire is situated southwest of Telluride and is a distinctive landmark as tourists drive the highway over Lizard Head Pass or as climbers hike to the top of San Juan peaks.

The snow sheds and support buildings of the Rio Grande Southern Railroad atop Lizard Head Pass. The railroad connected Durango, Dolores, Rico, and Telluride and was the route of the famous Galloping Goose, which carried mail, freight and a small number of passengers.

arm a few reluctant scabs that St. John had been educating. Or how *Examiner* Editor/Publisher George Sumner was relieved of publication for supporting striking union members (a local judge best known for drinking took over the paper's reins) and run out of town at gunpoint. Or how they handcuffed a union man to a telephone pole and it went out all over the country on the wire services. Telluride's colorful history began to come alive.

Anglo Exploration of the San Juans

Spaniards out of Santa Fe were the first Europeans to penetrate the mountains surrounding Telluride. Don Juan Maria de Rivera led the initial recorded expedition into this region in 1765, and pioneered what later became known as the Old Spanish Trail to California. It's likely that, following Rivera, many unrecorded forays were made into the San Juans by Spanish slave traders, prospectors and their Indian guides.

"In the 1820s Antoine St. Vrain and Thomas "Pegleg" Smith traveled north of Taos in 1824 and may possibly have entered the San Miguel Basin, boldly naming the Uncompahgre or perhaps the San Miguel, Smith's Fork. That name, however, didn't stick to either river."

The Dominguez-Escalante expedition of 1776 is credited with first naming the rivers of the region, except in the case of the San Miguel, which was named by the padres as the Rio de San Pedro, according to the journal of the expedition kept by Fray Silvestre Velez de Escalante. Subsequent maps by Humboldt and Pike, all based on the Dominguez-Escalante map, continued to call this river the San Pedro. However, a few years later the name San Miguel surfaced on a map by Warren A. Ferris in 1836, and for whatever reason it's the name that stuck. Perhaps Rivera dubbed it the Rio de San Miguel.

The name San Juan, applied to a principal tributary of the Colorado River by the Dominguez-Escalante party, was eventually applied to the far western ranges of the Southern Rockies, wherein the San Miguel Basin lies. By the start of the 19th century fur trapping mountain men had begun roaming into the San Juans and no doubt explored the San Miguel Basin.

In 1808-09 Jean Baptiste Champlain and two partners may have crossed the San Miguel while searching for a western route to Santa Fe around the San Juans. Their journal speaks of the perpetual snows of the high peaks. In the 1820s Antoine St. Vrain and Thomas "Pegleg" Smith traveled north of Taos in 1824 and may possibly have entered the San Miguel Basin, boldly naming the Uncompahgre or perhaps the San Miguel, Smith's Fork. That name, however, didn't stick to either river.

In 1828 Antoine Robidoux, a French trader from Missouri, established his Fort Uncompahgre trading post near the easiest ford of the Uncompahgre and Gunnison rivers, not far from the Ute Council Tree in present day Delta. While no record of his travels in the region has survived, it's highly likely he or some party from his small fort made it into the San Miguel Basin. In 1834, Robidoux bought rights and paid a good sum for a Spanish gold claim deep in the San Juans, the Cerro del Oro ("Mountain of Gold"). Early reports suggest that a Spanish arrastra existed along the upper San Miguel. Maybe Robidoux's lost mine was that very site.

And it's possible trapper James Ohio Pattie may have crossed the San Miguel in 1828 while traveling from Taos to Los Angeles. His journal suggests that he followed the Old Spanish Trail into the San Juans. According to Spanish court records, three of St. Vrain's men spent the winter of 1828-29 on the San Miguel River, and as a result St. Vrain was hauled into Spanish court on a customs and duty suit. And according to Uncle Dick Wootton, an early Colorado fur trader, Calvin Briggs traveled all over Colorado and may have touched the waters of the San Miguel while trapping beaver, in particular as a member of a group that left Bent's Fort in 1837.

But some reports of visitation to this area appear to be false. While a Forest

Trout Lake, which was used as a water supply for the Rio Grande Southern Railroad.

The Liberty Bell boarding house and tramway near Telluride. The Liberty Bell was one of the better-known mines in the area. It was also known for disaster. During one winter the Liberty Bell mine structures were swept away by an avalanche and rescuers arrived to help the injured. Unfortunately, another snowslide came down and covered many of the rescuers. In all, 18 people died that day.

A great labor conflict between 1899 and 1908 in Telluride resulted in numerous deaths and great suspicions. At the order of Colorado's Governor Peabody, Peabody's Fort was built in 1904 and manned by Colorado militia with a machine gun. The fort sat atop Imogene Pass between Telluride and Ouray.

FORT PEABODY

Perched above Imogene Pass at 13,365 feet, the small sentry post known as Fort Peabody was built in February and March 1904 during the height of statewide labor disturbances, when San Miguel County was under martial law. Bulkeley Wells, mine manager of the Smuggler-Union Mining Company and captain of Troop A, First Squadron Cavalry of the Colorado National Guard, ordered the stone redoubt built to prevent union miners and their sympathizers from entering the county, and to thwart deported men, classified as undesirable citizens, from returning home via the pass.

Troop A sentries, consisting of Wells' mine employees and cowboys from the west end of the county, occupied the post until martial law was revoked in the district on June 15, 1904. Some sources indicate the post may have been occupied until Troop A was mustered out in April 1905 at Wells' request. After this, his mining company employees may have occupied the post as sentries for the same purpose, until about 1908.

This was the highest sentry post in the state expressly built for the purpose of keeping a certain class of persons from entering a county. The redoubt derived its name from Cañon City businessman, James H. Peabody, who was governor.

Service monument at Lizard Head Pass suggests a party of fur trappers came through the watershed in 1833 and even spent part of a summer at Trout Lake, extensive research into the extant literature turns up no record of any Walton Expedition for the St. Louis Fur Co. in the 1830s, let alone a party of 60 men.

During the Mormon War of 1857-58, Capt. Randolph B. Marcy left Fort Bridger in what is now southwestern Wyoming on Nov. 24, 1857, with 65 men in an attempted winter crossing of the San Juans. After a 51-day march, perhaps crossing the San Miguel, they emerged from the mountain wilderness near Fort Massachusetts in the San Luis Valley.

In 1859 Capt. John N. Macomb led another survey party up from Santa Fe through the Dolores River watershed and the San Juan foothills along the route of the Old Spanish Trail, connecting New Mexico to Los Angeles, on his way to the junction of the Grand and Green rivers.

With the prospecting fever that followed the 1858-59 Pike's Peak Gold Rush, which really took place at Cherry Creek near the present site of Denver, the *Santa Fe Gazette* of 1860 printed an enthusiastic account of gold deposits in the San Juans, as did the *Rocky Mountain News*. That summer Charles Baker led a small party of gold seekers into Ute lands at the headwaters of the Animas River, the present site of the town of Silverton. There they organized 11 mining districts each con-

The Alta Mill complex near Telluride. Several historic structures remain near Alta, including one of the few "miner's hotels" in the state. Miner's hotels were more comfortable than the average boarding house.

The Corpse on Boomerang Road: Telluride's War on Labor, 1899-1908

By MaryJoy Martin

Time has silenced Telluride's labor conflict of a century ago, leaving in its wake only the story of the victors. Yet in the inscription on the Miners' Memorial in Lone Tree Cemetery, the vanquished whisper of the dark injustice that swept Telluride for a decade, an injustice perpetrated by powerful mine owners, governors, and the state militia.

At the center of Telluride's war on labor stood one corporation, the New England Exploration Company of Boston. In 1899, this company purchased the controlling interest in the Smuggler-Union Mine, and installed Arthur L. Collins as manager.

In order to squeeze more dividends from the low-grade ores of the Smuggler, Collins immediately implemented management practices that made piecework of mining, reduced the standard wage, endangered the lives of miners, and forced employees to board at the company's rooming houses. He had replaced union shift bosses with less experienced non-union men and had curtailed union activity on the property.

Collins's refusal to negotiate with the Telluride Miners' Union, a local of the Western Federation of Miners (WFM), led to a strike against the company in May 1901. He hired trigger-happy cowboys as mine guards, and brought in strikebreakers to work the mine. The guards harassed and assaulted union pickets daily, until their game turned deadly on July 3.

One picket named John Barthell, unarmed by all accounts, was shot dead when a delegation of union men approached the strikebreakers at shift change. Witnesses named a Collins foreman as the killer. The ensuing riot on the mountain lasted most of the morning, ending with three dead and six wounded.

Union president, Vincent St. John, was instrumental in bringing hostilities to an end. Most Telluride businessmen supported the union's demands for justice and fair wages, thus on July 6, 1901, the contenders reached an amicable settlement.

For the next year and a half, the relationship between the Miners' Union and the Smuggler Company stabilized. Yet the company despised St. John merely because he had an exceptional gift for organizing the miners, the local union gaining the second-largest membership in the WFM under his leadership. During his tenure, the Telluride local built a three-story brick hospital and union hall. The building still stands as a mute symbol of solidarity.

Law-abiding and personable, St. John firmly believed in nonviolence and the power of the strike and boycott. Although mine owners had nothing to fear from him, except his unswerving dedication to the rights of the worker, from the moment he had won the settlement, management determined to destroy him.

The mysterious disappearance of Smuggler employee William J. Barney turned into a tale of butchery, and St. John was named as the murderer, despite no evidence and no corpse. When Manager Collins was assassinated in November 1902, St. John was condemned as the killer.

Collins's replacement, Bulkeley Wells, took up the persecution of St. John as a sacred duty. Wells wanted the union leader hanging on the gallows and the union in ashes.

Although forced out of Telluride, with Pinkertons and gunmen hounding him, St. John's legacy remained: He had organized the millmen who demanded an eight-hour day in autumn of 1903. Once again the Smuggler Company's refusal to meet reasonable demands resulted in a strike.

With a new governor in office, the mine operators determined to restrict the growing power of the WFM. In Telluride, they immediately requested state militia to assist them in their scheme. Governor James Peabody provided troops, giving the mine operators the power of military might.

Union members carried out the Telluride strike of 1903-04 without any violation of the law, a fact repeatedly detailed in the Colorado National Guard reports of the commanding officer. Appointed as captain of his own Troop A, Manager Bulkeley Wells was granted free reign under martial law. He virtually broke the back of the Miners' Union through deportations, brutality, and flagrant violations of the union men's and their supporters' civil rights. The strike ended in destruction of the local union in June 1904. With the union gone, Wells and other managers granted an eight-hour day to the millmen because they knew the legislature was about to enact such a law.

On August 8, 1907, newspapers in Telluride declared the bones of Will Barney had been recovered from a shallow grave on Boomerang Hill, clear proof the Telluride Miners' Union had butchered him in 1901. Editors and Pinkertons claimed the union had slain several others also. Wells was triumphant.

Since that day, the belief that the Miners' Union was a pack of assassins and its victims numerous has endured for a century. Yet the alleged victims were, in fact, quite alive. The murder tales were merely part of the mine owners' plan to systematically destroy the Western Federation of Miners.

Used with permission from MaryJoy Martin, The Corpse on Boomerang Road: Telluride's War on Labor, 1899-1908; *Montrose, Colorado: Western Reflections Publishing Company, 2004.*

Clockwise from top: Extensive damage to homes and property in Telluride during the 1911 flood.

The view of downtown Telluride has not changed much over the years. Many of the buildings have retained their appearances; only the cars and paved streets indicate a 1960s setting.

The Ophir Loop near Telluride was an amazing feat of railroad engineering with numerous tight turns and wooden trestles. Today, only the grade of the Rio Grande Southern Railroad tracks is visible in places.

7249 Ophir Loop near Telluride, Colo.

Heritage tourism centered on the historic mining industry has become an important economic resource and four-wheel-drive trips are the best way to see the remnants of the mining complexes. Top left: The Smuggler Mill and Mine. Top right: Black Bear Mine boarding house. Bottom left: San Juan Jeep Tour at Black Bear Mine looking down into Telluride.

A pack train on the trail to a mine with its cargo of lumber in the early 1900s. Before the advent of the tramways, long lines of pack trains could be seen making their way up the mountains.

A hand-colored postcard depicting Pandora Park near Telluride with Bridal Veil Falls in the background and a wooden tram tower visible in the foreground.

taining some 200 claims, laid out three or four towns, and claimed the route from Baker's Park to Abiquiú, New Mexico, for a toll road.

Baker returned to Denver that fall, and rounded up a party of 100-300 men and women that winter to return to Baker's Park, arriving the next spring in Animas City — already a thriving supply camp of some 20 cabins and some 500 prospectors — 13 miles upriver from the present town of Durango. The women stayed at Camp Pleasant near the Hermosa Cliffs, while the men went on to Baker's Park and began digging without much luck. In the fall of 1861 Baker left to join the Confederate Army, and many miners became disillusioned at the remoteness of this earliest of San Juan mining camps.

The Utes and their Shining Mountains

The Utes, meanwhile, were being given the old Uncle Sam runaround. The first treaty in 1849 confined them to "their accustomed habitat" unless given permission to move, with agencies established for the Southern Utes at Taos (1851) and the Tabeguache Utes at Conejos (1861). Then a treaty in 1863 gave the Tabeguache Utes an area south from the Colorado River, west from the Sangre de Cristo Mountains, north of the Rio Grande River and east of the Uncompahgre River, which included Baker's Park, not that anyone seemed to notice or care.

But the San Luis Valley was too good as agricultural land to leave to the Indians, so with the help of Kit Carson another treaty was drawn up in 1868, moving the Utes further west to a line running from the present towns of Crested Butte on the north to Pagosa Springs on the south. Again the entire Animas River drainage was included in this new reservation. An agency for the Tabeguache band was set up 55 miles west of the present town of Saguache on a tributary of Cottonwood Creek. In 1870 several former members of the Baker party discovered gold in Arrastra Gulch, a tributary of the Animas River. By 1872 the rush was on, and some 2,000 miners fanned out across the San Juans hunting "color" in streams and washes.

The Utes protested the trespassing, and twice President Ulysses S. Grant ordered troops to remove prospectors. But the popular outcry for mineral development became unstoppable.

By 1873 Felix R. Brunot, president of the U.S. Board of Indian Commissioners, with the help of Otto Mears, convinced the Utes to cede the heart of the San Juans to the U.S. government in exchange for a narrow strip along the New Mexico and Utah borders (where the present Ute Mountain and Southern Ute reservations are located). The Utes received $25,000 a year, and the right to continue to hunt in the

San Juans as long as they remained peaceful. At the behest of the Department of Interior and the Department of War respectively, Ferdinand Vandeveer Hayden and Lt. George Montague Wheeler spent the summers of 1873, '74 and '75 directing four well-trained survey parties that mapped the Colorado Rockies, including the San Juans.

Ratified in the spring of 1874, the San Juan Purchase, as the treaty was called, "legally" opened the San Juans to the hordes of miners streaming into the rugged mountain canyons. That same year prospectors began placer mining up and down the San Miguel, which eventually led to a search for lodes in the headwater mountains. In August of 1875, John Fallon located the Sheridan vein in Marshall Basin, the first lode claim recorded in the area, and shipped one ton of silver ore to the smelter in Alamosa at a value of $2000.

THE LEGISLATURE CREATES NEW COUNTIES

On February 11, 1883, Montrose County came into being and the lower Basin was split off from Gunnison County. On February 27, 1883, the legislature created Uncompahgre County, and left the upper Basin as Ouray County. Three days later it changed its mind, and made Uncompahgre County back into Ouray County, and three-day-old Ouray County into San Miguel County.

When the dust had cleared, the San Miguel Basin was cut in two by a county line that separated the west end of Montrose County (the lower Basin) from San Miguel County (the upper Basin). The repeal of the Sherman Silver Purchase Act in 1893 was a bust that hurt this mining region, as it did most others, but not as badly as the pure silver camps like Aspen and Creede. Thanks to plentiful veins of gold the Basin rebounded, particularly in the boom of 1898-99. And it was the mining industry that continued to form the backbone of the Basin economy — silver, gold and lead in the upper Basin, and copper, vanadium and uranium in the lower Basin. In spite of periodic slumps, mines and mills survived in both ends of the Basin until the close of the Idarado Mine & Mill in 1978, and the collapse of the domestic uranium industry in the early 1980s.

TELLURIDE TOURISM

By the 1990s Telluride's tourism, real estate and construction boom had turned an old mining camp, barely scraping by, into a successful and chic destination ski resort and mountain festival magnet. The region's scenic allure had become its coin of the realm. Pure gold. Not the metallic kind, but the last of the nation's venues for unparalleled beauty and untrammeled natural vistas.

Which is why a book of postcards is a fitting way to celebrate not only the history of Telluride, but its unique claim as "The Most Beautiful Spot on Earth." ◆

Scenic beauty and heritage surround Telluride. Here is a view of the Smuggler-Union Mine.

A bird's-eye view of Telluride.

7408 Silverton-Ouray Toll Road, Colo.,   Mt. Abrams in distance

6722. ROCKY POINT, OURAY-SILVERTON STAGE ROAD, COLORADO.

SWITCHBACKS ON MILLION DOLLAR HIGHWAY RISING OUT OF OURAY, COLO.

Sanborn
W-1477

Hi Way near O

Today's Million Dollar Highway has evolved from its begin-
nings as a stage road in the 1880s to a modern highway.
Top and Right: The early Silverton-Ouray Stage Road.
Left: The stage road has improved to a gravel surface.
Bottom: The Million Dollar Highway in the 1950s.

MILLION DOLLAR HIGHWAY

No one knows for sure, but it could be that Otto Mears
found a million dollars in gold while
blasting for the toll road, or that the road was surfaced with
mine tailings that contained a million dollars' worth of gold,
or possibly that originally the road cost
a million dollars to build.

THE MILLION DOLLAR HIGHWAY: ROAD TO RED MOUNTAIN

BY NIK KENDZIORSKI

The Million Dollar Highway and the natural wonders that surround it have for decades drawn tourists to drive its rugged road and photograph its dramatic landscape. It is no accident that the road is prominently portrayed in early postcards. Stunning scenery and lofty, craggy peaks surround the Million Dollar Highway, but it was man's ingenuity and determination that carved a road through this magnificent mountain landscape. These early postcards are a testament to the will and determination not to let the terrain conquer the ambitions of miners and road builders. The postcards record this amazing accomplishment and beckon the traveler to follow this route and discover the historic 19th century mining landscape that surrounds the road.

The story of the Million Dollar Highway does not start with the arrival of Euro-Americans, but with Native Americans going back hundreds and even thousands of years ago. Throughout millennia, different cultural groups have traveled through the San Juan Mountains foraging for food or following game. These routes became well traveled and when the first Anglo miners came to the region to search for mineral riches, they, too, began to use these well-worn trails. Captain John Macomb described in an 1859 report that worn trails from all directions converged on the Pagosa hot springs. Early miners and explorers reported an "Indian" trail traversed Coal Bank Pass and descended into the Animas Canyon.

But it was the arrival of the Charles Baker prospecting party that first sparked interest in the San Juan Mountains and the possible riches locked in their lofty peaks. In 1860, Baker's party of 100 to 300 people arrived in Baker's Park, or what is now the town site of Silverton. They were searching for gold but not much of the precious metal was found and the prospecting party left the area disappointed. With the start of the Civil War, the area fell silent once more and development of the region's minerals would have to wait until after the war and the resulting influx of Civil War veterans in the 1870s. The rugged, isolated landscape was not the only difficulty to overcome when searching for gold.

The San Juan Mountains had been designated Ute land based on an 1868 treaty, and not until a second treaty was written to exclude the mineral-rich San Juan Mountains could extensive exploration and development occur safely. The second treaty was known as the San Juan Cession, or Brunot Agreement of 1873, and the

The Ironton Loops of the Million Dollar Highway drop out of Ironton Park with the Red Mountains in the background.

Early 1900s view of the Silverton-Ouray Stage Road. The route was rough and not for the weak of heart. This early route was spurred by the discovery of silver near Red Mountain Pass in 1881. The race was on to provide decent transportation for the mines.

1506 SILVERTON, ALTITUDE 9288 FT.,

AS SEEN FROM THE MILLION DOLLAR HIGHWAY, COLORADO

2894-30

The route between Silverton and Ouray did not get the name "Million Dollar Highway" until the mid 1920s, but the name caught on quickly and towns along the route were swift to pick up on its potential for community boosterism.

A group of early travelers stop to pose at Promontory Point on the stage road out of Ouray. Notice how the roadbed is only wide enough at this point for one stage to pass by. This is also the point where the cliff is steepest.

Promontory Point, Ouray Toll Road, Colo.

Utes originally opposed it, but Chief Ouray finally agreed to sign the treaty because the government promised to locate his lost son — a promise that was never kept. Utes reluctantly signed the treaty but agreed to give up only the mountaintops where the minerals were, not excellent hunting in the valleys of the Animas, La Plata, and Los Pinos rivers. The Anglo settlers did not honor this part of the treaty because they desired the valley bottoms to live and grow crops and livestock that would supply mining camps.

By the mid-1870s the mineral rush was on and mining camps began to spring up all over the mountains. A key factor in developing a prosperous mining region is reliable transportation routes, especially in such a rugged environment. In his article, "A Country of Tremendous Mountains: Opening the Colorado San Juans, 1870-1910," Duane Smith states, "Without an adequate transportation system, it would be difficult to ship ore to smelters, bring in needed equipment, reduce the cost of living, or entice investors to come."[1] Along with individual prospectors, roads and trails were some of the first things to appear in the mining areas. Well-maintained toll roads and railroads were essential to the survival of the isolated mining towns. However, this required large amounts of capital, engineering skill and pure determination to blast roads out of the steep and difficult landscape.

Entrepreneur Otto Mears was just the person who could accomplish this feat, and he eventually built or helped complete so many of the transportation routes in southwestern Colorado that he became known as the "Pathfinder of the San Juans." Mears is responsible for many routes in the San Juan Mountains including:

■ Silverton to Ouray toll road (Million Dollar Highway)
■ Dallas-San Miguel-Rico toll road
■ Silverton-Animas Forks-Mineral Point toll road
■ Rio Grande Southern Railroad
■ Silverton Railroad
■ Silverton, Gladstone and Northerly Railroad
■ Silverton Northern Railroad

Mears' roads, and his spectacular engineering feats shaped Southwest Colorado. The route that the Million Dollar Highway follows today is his most well-known accomplishment.

However, it would be misleading to state that Otto Mears constructed the entire route and that he alone built most of the routes in the mountains. On a number of roads in the region, Mears stepped in where others had failed. He had a knack for getting roads finished and then being able to make money from them, but how he operated the toll roads did not always earn him friends from the local population. Many local citizens thought his tolls excessive, and miners took other trails that went around the tollbooths, even if the route was more difficult. It was reported that Mears charged his highest toll to travel from Ouray to Silverton. The 24-mile trip cost $5 for a single-span team and $1 for each additional head of stock.[2]

The route of what was to become in later years the Million Dollar Highway is one of those that Mears took over after other companies failed to complete a road out of Ouray to the mines near Animas Forks, Howardsville, Silverton and Red Mountain Pass. Also, the route north from Ouray was through Ute territory and settlers were hesitant to travel this way for fears of hostilities between Utes and settlers. They wanted a road that would not lead through this territory. So, in 1880 the Ouray and San Juan Wagon Toll Road Company was formed and work began on a route south toward Silverton via established settlements such as Animas Forks, Eureka, and Silverton.[3]

THE RED MOUNTAIN DISTRICT

Rich discoveries of silver in 1881 in the Red Mountain District changed the planned route, because by 1882 there was an unprecedented boom in that district and the influx of people demanded good roads. The Ouray and San Juan Wagon Toll Road Company soon realized it was not up to the task of finishing the route to the district. Ouray County took over the Red Mountain extension of the main road that started 3½ miles south of Ouray at the Uncompahgre River crossing and they completed it to Ironton Park that summer.[4] It was in 1883 that Mears stepped in and completed the 3½ miles of the road from the town of Ouray to the Uncompahgre River crossing.

San Juan County, on the south side of Red Mountain Pass, was anxious to get in on the boom in the Red Mountain District and approached Mears about building a road from Silverton to the pass. Mears agreed and began construction of the road in July of 1884 and completed it by that November. However, there was a gap in the road between Silverton and Ouray. Ouray County's road ended in the town of Ironton and did not make it all the way to the top of Red Mountain Pass — the boundary between San Juan County and Ouray County. Mears was again approached by Ouray County to finish this segment of road and thereby link the towns of Ouray and Silverton.

The predicament for these communities was that Mears now controlled access to the booming mining district and according to many miners his tolls were too steep.

1569 Million Dollar Highway Between Ouray and Silverton, Colorado

The Western Slope's Great Thorofare thru the Switzerland of America to Mesa Verde National Park

During the mid 1920s the State of Colorado worked on the road between Silverton and Ouray and it is at this time that the route got its famous name, the "Million Dollar Highway." With the improved road, the opportunities for automobile travel and tourism through this rugged country also improved.
Top: Notice the stone guardrails along the road in the 1920s and 1930s.
Bottom: The Ironton Loops portion of the road is just before the highway enters the rugged and steep Uncompahgre Gorge.

IRONTON LOOPS AND RED MT. - MILLION DOLLAR HIGHWAY W-1069

The writer of this 1950s postcard asks, "How would you like to travel this road?" Many tourists continue to ask this question as they peer into the Uncompahgre Gorge.

The cost at which these roads were constructed had required lots of capital and Mears said the tolls were needed to recover his costs and to maintain the roads in good condition. The complaints and pressure continued to mount and in 1891 Mears sold his toll road to Ouray County.[5]

On the San Juan County side, the route was easier to navigate and Mears had constructed his toll road with the idea that in the future he would build a railroad from Silverton to the Red Mountain Mining District. In 1887, Mears began construction of the Silverton Railroad from Silverton to Red Mountain Pass along the route of his toll road and it soon became known as the Rainbow Route.[6] The railroad route was successful, but the Silver Crash of 1893 dealt a severe blow to the mines of the Red Mountain District and most closed. Because of the route's scenery, the train was able to survive with tourist traffic for a while, but by 1922 the railroad grade was abandoned and its right-of-way was deeded to San Juan County.[7] When the state began improving the gravel road between Ouray and Silverton, the highway route closely followed the railroad grade.

POSTCARDS AND AUTOMOBILE TRAVEL

The rise of the automobile in the early twentieth century allowed individuals to follow their own schedule, not the schedule of a train. Interest in improving roads also began to increase and movements were initiated around the country to create passable roads. Postcards were a way to advertise the beautiful scenery of the San Juan Mountains, and many of the postcards printed in this section are from the period following the increased improvement and construction that resulted from these "good roads" movements. The rugged route that Mears constructed to haul out mineral riches would now bring another industry to the southwest corner of Colorado — the tourist industry. *Highways of Colorado*, printed in 1912, provides a description of the early road between Ouray and Silverton:

"The road between Ouray and Silverton is a winding, steep road, rather narrow, often on solid ledge with some pretty steep grades. Is used more or less by automobiles. Built by Otto Mears in 1883, and considered a wonderful piece of engineering. Can hardly be recommended at present time for automobiling."[8]

The guide continues by giving a descriptive account of the route,

"Some of the greatest scenic wonders known to man can be viewed on the road from Ouray to Silverton and in the region thereabouts. Mountains on all sides rear their peaks far into the region of perpetual snows. Ouray and Silverton are the centers of a great mining district which has produced many millions…Tourists who do not care to undertake the 'scenic highway' by automobile can stop at Ouray and go by stage or team to the various mining camps. Days can be spent here viewing the great works of nature."[9]

Postcards and guides like *Highways of Colorado* provided descriptions of the region and helped to draw tourists. The tourist roads would become a source of community pride and in 1916, the county of Ouray together with the state, spent $8,000 to improve the first two miles of Otto Mears' old toll road south of the town of Ouray.[10] In 1920, with $50,000 in Federal Aid Project money, the state began work on the road north of Bear Creek Falls, including a 200-foot-long, 17-foot-wide tunnel. Workers clung to the side of the mountain above a 200-foot sheer drop to the canyon floor and bore a hole out of solid rock. Navajo Indians were part of this group and it was their job to clear the tunnel.[11]

As the tourism industry expanded in Colorado, the Million Dollar Highway was to become a major touring destination for daring drivers. As more tourists flocked to the area, in 1924 the Colorado Highway Department started to improve and expand on Mears' old toll road. It was at this time that state engineers redesigned the 12-mile stretch between Ouray and Red Mountain Pass and began to widen and place gravel on the roadbed. In July of 1924 the state held a dedication ceremony at the top of Red Mountain Pass and officially dedicated the Durango-Silverton-Ouray road. By 1930, according to the Department of Highways, the road alternated between gravel and surfaced road and the highway was eventually extended to the New Mexico state line in 1935.[12]

NAMING "THE MILLION DOLLAR HIGHWAY"

The "Million Dollar Highway" is a name that has become synonymous with Highway 550 from Durango to Ouray and sometimes even from the New Mexico state line to the town of Montrose. Postcards from the 1920s until today have captions that tout a certain town or attraction that is on the "Million Dollar Highway." The name was a great marketing tool and town boosters wanted to be associated with the name. However, the name originally applied exclusively to the 12 miles between Ouray and Red Mountain Pass that was improved by the state in 1924.

How the highway got its name has been one of myth and legend. Popular stories behind the name include a claim that Otto Mears found a million dollars in gold while blasting for the toll road, or that the road was surfaced with mine tailings that contained a million dollars' worth of gold, and possibly that originally the road cost a million dollars to build. The most plausible, but less romantic version is attributed to a contractor stating, "the million-dollar highway we're building" after considering what it would take to finish the improvements to the road for the Department of Highways in the 1920s.[13] It is a phrase that caught on quickly with the public and was even published in an article in the May 1923 issue of *Colorado Highways*. No matter the origin of the name, it remains popular today with locals and visitors alike.

Early 1900s panoramic view looking south up the gorge toward Mount Abrams. Imagine looking up the gorge from this point knowing you still had that entire rough road ahead of you.

Two stages make their way along the narrow toll road. It is at this point where Otto Mears collected his toll for use of the route. Many miners and travelers complained about the amount of toll that Mears charged. They felt it was excessive for such a rough road.

Tunnel constructed in 1924 on the Million Dollar Highway in Uncompahgre Gorge between Ouray and Silverton.

7408   Silverton-Ouray Toll Road, Colo.,   Mt. Abrams in distance

Top right: Automobiles travel the road in the 1920s with the safety of stone guard rails.

The people who rode stage coaches along the early toll road did not have the luxury of stone guard rails to protect them from going over the cliff edge.

It took many years before the road between Ouray and Silverton was paved. However, the graded, gravel roadbed was a vast improvement over the original toll road. It allowed the automobile to make a safer and more comfortable journey between Ouray and Silverton.

Even though most of the mines of the Red Mountain District had long been closed, the Million Dollar Highway was to become important in hauling valuable ore once again. The highway took on additional significance during World War II and the ensuing Cold War era.

As the United States Army developed atomic weapons under the top-secret Manhattan Project, large deposits of necessary uranium ores were located across southwestern Colorado. From 1943 to 1945, the success of the Manhattan Project depended on clear roads to transport materials in and out of southwestern Colorado to the refining facility in Grand Junction. State maintenance crews, driving a fleet of 60 trucks, kept the highway over Red Mountain Pass open year-round so that the Army could haul sulfuric acid and other supplies from Grand Junction to support facilities in Durango.[14]

A tourist makes their way down the switchbacks from Red Mountain Pass on the Million Dollar Highway in a vintage 1957 Chevrolet station wagon with matching camper trailer. The road has been improved to a point where the family station wagon and camper can be pulled through this beautiful mountain scenery.

"THE ROUTE BETWEEN OURAY AND SILVERTON HAS SOME OF THE MOST DANGEROUS AVALANCHES IN THE COUNTRY. SIXTY NAMED AVALANCHES CROSS THE HIGHWAY."

Keeping the road open year round has never been an easy task and has had deadly consequences for some travelers.

Several postcards in this chapter reveal some of the winter conditions, but they do not illustrate all the dangers of traveling in the winter. From the time that the route was established to the mines in the Red Mountain area until today, the dangers of winter and keeping the road open year-round have posed great trouble for travelers. The mid-1920s put the road under the supervision of the State of Colorado, but it was not until 1935 that they were able to keep the road open year-round on a fairly regular basis. The route between Ouray and Silverton has some of the most dangerous avalanches in the country. Sixty named avalanches cross the highway. From the time the mines opened in the early 1880s, deaths from precarious winter conditions were a part of traveling Otto Mears' toll road and the route that the Million Dollar Highway follows today.

Remnants of a mine and its supporting structures were once visible along the Million Dollar Highway. Some mine buildings have disappeared due to road projects, vandalism, and the ravages of time. Today, the Red Mountain Task Force and its partners are trying to preserve and stabilize the mining heritage along the Million Dollar Highway.

AVALANCHES AND "THE WHITE DEATH"

The cemeteries at Silverton and Ouray attest, unfortunately, to the many victims who have died from avalanches in the region. An early victim of avalanche danger was Thomas Brennan, who was killed with ten mules in an 1883 snowslide between the Yankee Girl Mine and Sweetville;

"A deadly slide made its power felt when a man and ten mules perished in its icy embrace. The snow had been falling continuously for several days and was heavy on the mountainsides. February 2nd was an unusually warm day and at about noon, the Stafford muletrain was packing ore from the Yankee Girl Mine to Sweetville. While on the trail to the mine, the procession was engulfed in a snowslide which crashed down from the rocky cliffs 300 feet above the trail. Tom Brennan, Jim Barr and thirteen mules disappeared in the snow, ice and debris…The men from the Yankee Girl Mine were soon on the ground with shovels, working their hardest to rescue the unfortunate men and animals. About half an hour after the slide had run, lying alongside a dead mule, Jim Barr was found buried under six feet of snow, but still alive. The fifty men continued digging feverishly, looking for Brennan, but he was not found until the next day."[15]

On the south side of Red Mountain Pass, the town of Chattanooga was the main supply point to the Red Mountain mines before the train arrived in the late 1880s. The route from Silverton to Chattanooga was difficult, but from the town to the mines it was more dangerous. In 1883, John "Jack" Dolan was killed in a snowslide in Mill Gulch near Chattanooga;

"John met death at 3:30 on a Thursday afternoon, the victim of a 'small' snowslide. He and two companions were packing grub and supplies from Chattanooga up Mill Gulch to the Silver Crown Mine. When about half a mile up the gulch, a small slide came down, caught Jack and another man and carried them down the mountain about fifty yards. The other man was not injured, but Jack was dead though rescued immediately after the slide."[16]

John Dolan's gravesite went unmarked for more than a hundred years on the mountainside near what was once the town of Chattanooga. In 1994, Jack Pfertsch of the U.S. Forest Service led the effort in placing tombstones at the site for Jack Dolan and Harry Hall.[17] The Forest Service continues to maintain the plot by putting a small wrought iron fence around the tombstones in the summer and taking it down during the winter.

The winter of 1885-86 produced numerous slides and a number of deaths. The Red Mountain district recorded the death of five miners on January 23, 1886. The local newspaper reported that the winter was particularly difficult and that for the

Winter in the San Juan Mountains and along the Million Dollar Highway can be treacherous. Avalanches, especially between Silverton and Ouray, can be a severe hazard to motorists and a number of people have been killed or injured. This is a winter scene along the Million Dollar Highway.

An avalanche covers the Million Dollar Highway, circa 1930s.

BOARDING HOUSE AVALANCHES IN THE SAN JUAN MOUNTAINS

RESEARCH BY FREDA PETERSON

Though thousands of miners came to the San Juans to mine gold and silver between 1860 and 1920, only a very few historic miners' cabins and boarding houses remain. Many structures burned, but a number were destroyed by avalanches, which makes the existing structures valuable as historic and cultural resources. From the book *Death in the Snow* by Freda Peterson (2003), which is an analysis of all the people who died in area avalanches and were buried in the Silverton, Colorado, cemetery, these facts emerge on the devastation that avalanches wreaked to boarding houses and bunkhouses. Boarding houses crushed by snow included:

SAMPSON MINE NEAR GLADSTONE
March 10, 1884
Sampson Mine Boarding House

The spring slide killed "Long John" Radamacher and demolished the recently completed Sampson concentration and smelting works, all the new machinery, boarding house, stable and lower end of the tramway. Author Freda Peterson writes, "Radamacher and Charley Herrick were both in the boarding house when the avalanche hit. Herrick was recovered alive, but Long John's body was not found for a month. He was in the very room he had occupied when the slide hit, and in his mouth, unbroken, was the pipe he had been smoking when swept into eternity."

SAMPSON MINE NEAR GLADSTONE
January 1886
Sampson Mine Boarding House

From the *Silverton Weekly Miner* of January 26, 1906

In January 1886 Olaf Arvid Nelson, his wife, Lousia, and their children, five year old Anna and two year old Oscar, lived in the boarding house near the Sampson Mill. After a San Juan storm had dumped several feet of snow on the mountains, the family was sitting together after supper, Olaf, holding the baby, Oscar was in a rocking chair. Suddenly a thundering avalanche of snow, ice, rock and timber swept down the mountainside annihilating everything in its path including the boarding house. Olaf managed to pull the stovepipe out of the debris inside the smashed structure and pushed it up through the cement like snow which covered them. He succeeded in working a hole large enough to get himself through, then was able to rescue Louisa, who was six months pregnant, and their daughter, Anna, out of the wreckage. Olaf then climbed down into the wrecked cabin to look for the baby and discovered heavy timbers had fallen across the arms of the rocking chair and pinned little Oscar there, unhurt. He was so firmly wedged, Olaf had to cut away the back of the chair to get the baby out. Olaf's quick thinking and his marvelous physical strength had saved him and his family from awful deaths. Their escape from the tragedy was nothing short of a miracle.

SHENANDOAH MINE SNOWSLIDE, CUNNINGHAM GULCH
St. Patrick's Day 1906
Highland Mary Mine Boarding House

In places the snow was 150 feet deep. "The slide struck like a thunderbolt as the twenty-one men were finishing supper in the boarding house." "The Iowa Mill was knocked to pieces and the Highland Mary Boarding House and engine room were swept away."

Twelve miners died that day and nine managed to escape. The dead included Bert Albert, Flake Blanton, Emil Bro, Peter Carlberg, Dominic Ferraglio, Nels Gustafson, Gus Heise, Addison J. "Ed" Kirk, Antonio Oberto, Jesse Shaw, Jacob Theobald and Giacomo

LAST CHANCE MINE ON KING SOLOMON MOUNTAIN
St. Patrick's Day, 1906
Unity Tunnel Boarding House
Last Chance Boarding House
And a cabin

At the Unity Tunnel "a slide destroyed the boarding house but most of the men were working in the mine, and the only man injured was a cook, Nels Hansen, who suffered a broken leg. The slide continued down the mountain, struck the Last Chance workings, a part of the same property where Italians were employed. The bunkhouse was destroyed and Rodolfo Paveglio was carried away to his death. . . . Below the Last Chance the slide struck the cabin occupied by Elmer Johnson and his wife, near the bottom of Arrastra Gulch. After turning the cabin over several times the slide landed Mrs. Johnson, apparently uninjured, several hundred feet from the starting point."

Silver Wing Bunkhouse near Animas Forks
St. Patrick's Day, 1906

Bunkhouse destroyed and George Abbott and "Lucky Bill" Thompson killed.

Sunlight Bunkhouse near Animas Forks
St. Patrick's Day, 1906

Bunkhouse hit by an avalanche and Joseph Walker killed.

Tom Moore Boarding House Slide
December 16, 1908

A severe storm began on a Monday night. "One early Wednesday afternoon at the Tom Moore Boarding House two miles above Eureka, Bill Mundell was sitting near the furnace in the northwest corner of the basement. A monstrous snowslide hit the building on that very corner then crashed through into the basement. Hit by flying timber, wreckage and the full weight of the snow, Bill was instantly killed then buried under the mass of snow, timber and debris. No one else was hurt and the building was struck only on that corner."

Gold King Mine Boarding House near Gladstone
March 11, 1911

Men had been laid off a few weeks before at the Gold King Mine, and Francis Schnee left her baby daughter with her mother and went to Silverton to look for work. She never saw her daughter or her mother again as both the

grandmother and the daughter and another woman were killed by a slide, which destroyed the kitchen on the ground floor and also swept away Samson Hore who had been in the upper story of the boarding house. He was found 300 feet down the gulch covered with three room partitions and twelve feet of snow.

Edited and used with permission from Freda Peterson, Death in the Snow; Excerpts from The Story of Hillside Cemetery, Silverton, Colorado *(Silverton: Ferell Publications, 2003).*

Winter is a spectacular time in the San Juan Mountains and more and more Americans want to recreate in the mountains during this time of the year. Keeping the road open all year round, especially in winter, is a challenge for the road crews and it was not until 1935 that they were able to do this on a regular basis.

MILLION DOLLAR HIGHWAY NEAR SILVERTON, COLO.

Rugged beauty and deep snow along the Million Dollar Highway.

Another danger along the highway is falling ice from cliffs at the edge of the road. In the past, motorists and their cars have been hit by large chunks of ice.

first time in memory, slides were being reported in places that had not avalanched before.[18]

Another death in 1886 occurred following the recovery of victims from an avalanche in the Red Mountain area. Barney McGinn froze to death near Bear Creek Falls,

"Barney, an old time San Juan miner, was frozen near Bear Creek Falls. He and several other men were hauling the bodies of snowslide victims, Wirt Randall, Frank Graham, John Hendrickson and Phil Foster, to Ouray for burial...Barney had stopped at the toll gate for a few drinks while the other men went on ahead. When he resumed his journey alone, he eventually became exhausted and froze to death...The *Ouray Solid Muldoon* newspaper was kinder to Barney in its report, stating that he had dug all night in the snowslide rescue attempt, then started to Ouray to get help. He collapsed half a mile north of the toll gate, was brought down to the Sanderson Hotel in Ouray and died somewhat later...There were scores of death-dealing slides in the winter of 1885-86, and no accurate count could ever be made of how many died. Slides occurred in places where they had never before run and it was said there was no place in the mountains where a slide could not occur."[19]

Not all slides were able to claim a victim. One person was able to survive the dangerous Riverside Slide and read his own obituary. During the winter of 1897 John Bell carried the mail between Red Mountain and Ouray.

There were no witnesses when he was caught in the infamous Riverside Slide. He was unconscious 12 hours in a cave-like aperture of the river, covered with snow, but dry because the snow had dammed the river. After regaining consciousness it was only by unbelievable perseverance and hard work that he managed to free himself from the mountain of snow over him.[20]

Most people are not as lucky as Bell, especially when it comes to the Riverside Slide. That slide not only caused death to victims caught in its grip, but it also made travel difficult in general. In the early days of travel through the Uncompahgre Gorge, the Riverside Slide often required men to dig a tunnel 600 feet long in order to keep the road open. Until a snowshed was constructed over the highway in 1985[21], the Riverside Slide was an extremely dangerous spot following storms in the winter,

"On Sunday morning, March 3, 1963, Rev. Marvin Hudson, with his two daughters, Amelia, 17, and Pauline, age 15, left Ouray to drive to Silverton where he would conduct church services. His family and Silverton residents tried, to no avail, to discourage him from making the trip because of the howling blizzard which was raging at the time...The East Riverside slide had run at about 4:00 that morning, and was being cleared by the State Highway plow. Rev. Hudson drove around the plow, found he needed more traction, so he got out and jacked up the car to put a chain on a rear wheel. The girls stayed in the car and the snowplow driver started to pull the Hudson car back down the road out of the dangerous area…The East Riverside slide struck again. The air blast pushed the heavy snowplow back down the road, and when the air cleared the highway and canyon were filled with snow. The car and its occupants had disappeared…The body of Rev. Hudson was found a week later, 280 feet from where he was last seen. The car was 600 feet from the point of impact, and 17 year old Amelia was under it. Pauline was not found until May 30th when relatives found her in the melting slide debris."[22]

$$\blacklozenge \; \blacklozenge \; \blacklozenge$$

Even though the snowshed has been built to protect travelers, the Riverside Slide is still dangerous. Locals felt that the shed was too short and a fight with the Colorado Department of Transportation ensued. However, a lack of funding to lengthen the shed brought the conflict to a close and the shed was not expanded. The danger of the Riverside Slide and the shortcomings of the shed would be evident in 1992 with the death of a CDOT snowplow driver just outside the protection of the snow shed.

Travelers and miners were not the only ones to fall victim to the monstrous slides that flowed into Uncompahgre Gorge. The men who have risked their lives to keep the Million Dollar Highway open during the winter have also lost their lives. Three Colorado Department of Transportation snowplow drivers have died since 1970 while keeping the road clear — Robert Miller in 1970, Terry Kishbaugh in 1978, and Eddie Imel in 1992. A stone memorial has been placed in Uncompahgre Canyon along the road to commemorate the service of these men.

Over the years, much has been learned about the conditions that make it likely that an avalanche will run, and the Colorado Department of Transportation staff knows where the major slides, such as the Riverside Slide, occur. CDOT can then set off explosives that bring down snow in a controlled manner while they have the highway closed. However, dangers still exist from avalanches and other elements. Several years ago, a car was driving the Million Dollar Highway in the Uncompahgre Gorge and a large chunk of ice the size of a basketball fell from a cliff above and crashed through the car's windshield on the passenger side. Luckily no one was in the passenger's seat and the person driving was not seriously injured, except for some cuts from broken glass. As is the case with Mother Nature, it is hard to control every possible hazard.

The development of the highway has an interesting history and the Million Dollar Highway is an important cultural and economic resource for the region. Preservation of its historic sites and landscape is important to the survival of the old mining towns that used to rely on it to haul out valuable ore.

With its hot springs, dancing, and music, Pinkerton Springs would have been a nice place to stop on a winter day in the 1920s and 1930s. However, this stop along the Million Dollar Highway was short-lived and only the springs remain today.

Winter vista from the Durango-Silverton Highway looking toward Twilight Peak, circa 1920s. Eventually, this stretch of road would also become known as part of the Million Dollar Highway.

MILLION DOLLAR HIGHWAY AT LIME CREEK, NEAR DURANGO, COLO.

The mining industry and landscape along the Million Dollar Highway has evolved over the years, as has the road itself. This 1930s postcard shows a section of the highway that is no longer part of today's highway alignment. It is along the Old Lime Creek Road, which is still gravel and unpaved. The stone guard rails remain along this old section of the highway.

1566—Red Mountain on the Million Dollar Highway

Between Ouray and Silverton, Colo.   5672-29-N

Travelers along the Million Dollar Highway have always been captivated by the Red Mountains and their brilliant red hues.

THE RED MOUNTAIN TASK FORCE AND THE TRUST FOR PUBLIC LAND

Today, the Red Mountain Task Force, in partnership with the Trust for Public Land, is trying to preserve the mountain viewshed and historic structures that surround the road and that are illustrated in these postcards. The effort to save this astonishing scenery and the historic structures, which were connected to the outside world by the Million Dollar Highway, had its roots in 1997. This was the year that the Fort Lewis College Office of Community Services in Durango received a grant to create a historic preservation plan for the San Juan Skyway, which is a 232-mile loop that traverses the San Juan Mountains and includes the stretch of the Million Dollar Highway between Silverton and Ouray.[23]

During the summer of 1998, the directors of the San Juan and Ouray County Historical Societies along with other historic preservationists joined the Office of Community Services to inventory historic structures in the area of Red Mountain Pass. It was during this survey that they realized many of these structures and the land around them were held in private hands on what appeared to be public lands. The group decided something needed to be done. A meeting brought about 35 people together to discuss the situation and in the end 15 volunteers formed what was to be called the Red Mountain Task Force.[24]

The idea formed from this meeting was to try to buy the privately held mining claims from willing sellers and then put the property back into the public domain. It was a bold and complicated task that required help. In 1998 the task force approached the Trust for Public Land and informed them of its idea to buy the private land. Complex issues needed to be addressed, but TPL was supportive of the plan. To buy the mining claims required numerous answers including liability concerns over cleanup at old mining claims.[25]

As the idea gained momentum in 1999, the Red Mountain Task Force, the Trust for Public Land, and the Forest Service released a plan to purchase 11,000 acres of old mining claims in the Red Mountain area.[26] Of course, funding such an ambitious project was the next question. However, at this time, the Land and Water Conservation Fund was receiving increased appropriations from Congress. The Fund receives royalties from offshore oil and gas leases to acquire lands for conservation and it is up to Congress to appropriate money from this fund. The money estimated to purchase the mining claims in the Red Mountain area totaled $15 million and the LWCF was the best funding option, with Great Outdoors Colorado and the State Historic Fund contributing as well.[27]

Public and community support would be crucial in securing funding for the project. Landowners willing to sell their property came forward and a maker of outdoor gear, Black Diamond Equipment, Ltd., added its support to the project. One of the largest property owners in the Red Mountain area was the Idarado Mining Company, which was formed in 1939 and operated mines in the area until 1978. They were looking to sell much of their property and preferred to have the land in the public domain.[28]

Of course, as with many mining sites in the West, liability with hazardous mining waste was a key issue to acquiring these properties. For many people, the sight of mining waste is one, and possibly the only, of the main indications that they are looking at a historic mine. Time and weather have reduced mine structures and the human-built environment to ruins. Mining waste lasts a long time and marks the site of great activity, but also creates problems for public health. The groups involved with preserving the Red Mountain landscape received much needed help when the regional office of the Environmental Protection Agency assured them that it would address the liability associated with the mining waste in the Red Mountain area.

"… CHANGES ALONG THE ROAD HAVE BEGUN TO ALTER ITS APPEARANCE WITHOUT TAKING THE ROUTE'S HISTORY INTO ACCOUNT."

Important components of the project were now in place, however, in 2000 one of the most significant aspects of the project failed to come through — funding from the Land and Water Conservation Fund. The Red Mountain Task Force organized a grass-roots campaign to secure the funding and sent letters to Colorado's Congressional representatives and senators.[29] The campaign worked and $5 million was secured for the project that year and more importantly it put the Red Mountain area on many people's map. The effort not only secured funding, but also attention to important cultural resources.

The project had gained momentum and by the next fiscal year the National Trust for Historic Preservation named the Red Mountain Mining District as one of its most endangered historic places and to date, an excess of $14 million has been raised.[30] The Red Mountain Task Force and the Trust for Public Land brought

A lone automobile makes its way along the Million Dollar Highway, described on the back-side of the postcard as "the most magnificent mountain drive in the world."

Today, towns like Silverton (pictured), Ouray, and Durango rely on the tourists that drive the Million Dollar Highway as an economic replacement to the mining industry.

thousands of acres of Idarado mining claims into public ownership and was in line to receive more LWCF funding. In addition to Idarado mining claims, the partnership has been able to bring hundreds more acres into public ownership from private individuals willing to sell their property for the project. Acquiring land is not the only accomplishment of the Red Mountain Task Force.

Several historic structures have been stabilized and more are scheduled to be stabilized, a $600,000 scenic overlook has been constructed with signs interpreting the Red Mountain Mining District, and several miles of historic trails are now available to the public. Recently, the partnership was able to secure title to the privately held 805-acre Ironton Park and save it from possible development. In the same area, Ouray County owns and protects the historic town site of Ironton and 110 acres to the west of the site. The Ironton Park purchase has stunning scenery and its rare wetlands have been added to the Uncompahgre National Forest. The partnership continues to this day to work to bring more mining claims under the protection of the U.S. Forest Service and Ouray County for the enjoyment of the American public.

Efforts to protect the landscape along the Million Dollar Highway like the Red Mountain Project are important, because changes along the road have begun to alter its appearance without taking the route's history into account. In the mid-1990s, the Colorado Department of Transportation was going to alter the highway tunnel located near Ouray. Several images of this tunnel are shown in this chapter shortly after it was completed. It is an important historical resource of the Million Dollar Highway. CDOT was going to cut through the tunnel, but community support saved it and now tourists travel through the tunnel exactly as people did in 1924, the date of its completion. Highway projects need to be watched to save the structures and landscape that are portrayed in these early postcards.

Just like the historic mining sites and the Million Dollar Highway, the postcards collected by Nina Heald Webber are an important resource to this community and a connection to the past. In the 21st century where mountain sprawl and development threaten the Million Dollar Highway corridor, it is significant to have this collection of 19th and 20th century postcards to hold onto a vision of this stunning route. ◆

There is only one tunnel along the route of the Million Dollar Highway and it was completed in 1924. Today, tourists along the highway can still travel through this tunnel near Ouray which is relatively unchanged since it was constructed. Some alterations occurred to deal with larger automobiles. In the 1990s the Colorado Department of Transportation wanted to eliminate the tunnel, but public outcry saved the tunnel from destruction and allowed for future generations to travel through.

Through the Tunnel.
"Million Dollar" highway.
109

TUNNEL ON MILLION DOLLAR HIGHWAY, NEAR DURANGO, COLO.

BIBLIOGRAPHY

Brown, Robert L. *An Empire of Silver.* Denver: Sundance Publications, Ltd., 1984.

Clifford, Hal. *Laying Claim to Red Mountain, Land & People.* The Trust for Public Land. Volume 15, Number 1, Spring 2003. pp. 24-30.

Gregory, Marvin and P. David Smith. *The Million Dollar Highway: Colorado's Most Spectacular Seventy Miles.* Ouray, Colorado: Wayfinder Press, 1986.

Highways of Colorado: Official Guide & Tour Book. Issued under authority of The Colorado State Highway Commission. Denver: The Clason Map Co., 1912.

Highways to the Sky: A Context and History of Colorado's Highway System. Report submitted to Colorado Department of Transportation by Associated Cultural Resource Experts. May 31, 2002.

Kaplan, Michael. *Otto Mears: Paradoxical Pathfinder.* Silverton, Colorado: San Juan Country Book Co., 1982. (Michael David Kaplan, "Otto Mears: Colorado's Transportation King," Ph.D. dissertation, University of Denver, 1975).

Marshall, John and Jerry Roberts. *Living (and dying) in Avalanche Country: Stories from the San Juans of Southwestern Colorado.* Published by author, 1993.

Peterson, Freda Carley. *Death in the Snow: Excerpts from The Story of Hillside Cemetery.* Silverton, Colorado: Ferrell Publications, 2003.

Reynolds, Branson. *One Drive in a Million: A mile-by-mile guide to the Million Dollar Highway and the San Juan Skyway.* Durango, Colorado: Desert Dolphin, Inc., 1994.

Sloan, Robert E. and Carl A. Skowronski. *The Rainbow Route: An Illustrated History of The Silverton Railroad, The Silverton Northern Railroad and The Silverton, Gladstone & Northerly Railroad.* Denver: Sundance Publications, Ltd., 1975.

ENDNOTES

[1] William Wyckoff and Lary M. Dilsaver, eds., *The Mountainous West: Explorations in Historical Geography* (Lincoln: University of Nebraska Press, 1995), p. 99.

[2] Robert E. Sloan and Carl A. Skowronski, *The Rainbow Route* (Denver: Sundance Publications, Ltd., 1975), p. 43.

[3] Marvin Gregory and P. David Smith, *The Million Dollar Highway: Colorado's Most Spectacular Seventy Miles* (Ouray, Colorado: Wayfinder Press, 1986), p. 58.

[4] Ibid., p. 58.

[5] Ibid., p. 59.

[6] Robert E. Sloan and Carl A. Skowronski, *The Rainbow Route* (Denver: Sundance Publications, Ltd., 1975), p. 45.

[7] Marvin Gregory and P. David Smith, *The Million Dollar Highway: Colorado's Most Spectacular Seventy Miles* (Ouray, Colorado: Wayfinder Press, 1986), p. 59.

[8] *Highways of Colorado: Official Guide & Tour Book* (Denver: The Clason Map Co., 1912), p. 117.

[9] Ibid., p. 117.

[10] *Highways to the Sky: A Context and History of Colorado's Highway System* (Report submitted to Colorado Department of Transportation by Associated Cultural Resource Experts, May 31, 2002), p. 11-4.

[11] Ibid., p. 11-4.

[12] Ibid., p. 11-4.

[13] Marvin Gregory and P. David Smith, *The Million Dollar Highway: Colorado's Most Spectacular Seventy Miles* (Ouray, Colorado: Wayfinder Press, 1986), p. 16.

[14] *Highways to the Sky: A Context and History of Colorado's Highway System* (Report submitted to Colorado Department of Transportation by Associated Cultural Resource Experts, May 31, 2002), p. 11-5.

[15] Freda Carley Peterson, *Death in the Snow: Excerpts from The Story of Hillside Cemetery* (Silverton, Colorado: Ferrell Publications, 2003), p. 18.

[16] Ibid., p. 35.

[17] Ibid., p. 36.

[18] Ibid., pp. 38 and 39.

[19] Ibid., p. 75.

[20] Ibid., p. 143.

[21] Branson Reynolds, *One Drive in a Million: A mile-by-mile guide to the Million Dollar Highway and the San Juan Skyway* (Durango, Colorado: Desert Dolphin, Inc., 1994), p. 34.

[22] Freda Carley Peterson, *Death in the Snow: Excerpts from The Story of Hillside Cemetery* (Silverton, Colorado: Ferrell Publications, 2003), pp. 145 and 146.

[23] Hal Clifford, *Laying Claim to Red Mountain, Land & People* (The Trust for Public Land, Volume 15, Number 1, Spring 2003), p. 27.

[24] Ibid., p. 27.

[25] Ibid., p. 28.

[26] Ibid., p. 29.

[27] Ibid., p. 29.

[28] Ibid., p. 29.

[29] Ibid., p. 29.

[30] Ibid., p. 30.

APPENDIX A:
A PERSPECTIVE ON POSTCARDS

By Lynne R. Carpenter

T he very nature of postcards separates them from commissioned photos, because postcards were purchased not only as collectibles to be cherished, but also to be sent to treasured friends and relatives, as well. Postcard use in the early twentieth century is a fascinating study.

Postcards have a long and interesting history that begins over 100 years ago in the Austro-Hungarian Empire. Dr. Emmanuel Hermann proposed a postal card that was accepted by the director-general of the Austrian Post on October 1, 1869. The product was termed a "Correspondence Card." The original European postcard was the size of an envelope with the title, name of the postal district, and coat-of arms of the country on the front. The back of the card was left blank for communication.

The impetus for the creation of the postcard lies in the rigid customs dictating the manner in which nineteenth century correspondence transpired. In addressing a letter to another individual, certain forms of communication had to be followed. "One must first inquire after the health of the recipient and state one's own condition of health. One had to ask after various other members of the family and perhaps give a bit of local news."[1] In addition, the implements required for the creation of a letter (ink, pen, stationery, sealing wax, seal), and the postage for a letter meant for expense to the sender. In some countries the postal charge was paid by the recipient rather than the sender, which placed a future obligation upon the writer to make the letter worth the money.[2] Thus the creation of the much-simplified correspondence card was an issue of utility.

American interest in postcards followed the European trend. Though one enterprising soul copyrighted a private postcard in 1861, John P. Charlton of Philadelphia, Pennsylvania, devised the earliest private postcard, but transferred his copyright to H. Lipman, also of Philadelphia.[3] The Lipman cards were very simple with "Lipman's Postal Card" in the upper left corner and a patent applied for statement below. The earliest example

Early 20th century agricultural display at the Colorado, New Mexico Fair in Durango, Colorado. This postcard helped to promote the bountiful and fertile land of the community.

This 1914 postcard hoped to find everyone in good health. This was one of the customs of early 1900s postcard correspondence.

Early 20th century postcards helped promote the cultural resources and community pride of a town or region. Top: Visitors to Mesa Verde National Park and Spruce Tree House, circa 1910s. Bottom: A horse race at the Spanish Trails Fiesta in Durango, Colorado in the 1930s. This celebration was meant to display the true western spirit.

of a Lipman card is dated October 25, 1870. Lipman's cards were popular until the U.S. government issued postcards in 1873, although the Postmaster General had put forth the idea of a card as early as 1870. Postcards were also used as early as 1873 as promotional mailers for hotels, resorts and businesses.[4]

While 1865 and 1872 were landmark dates for government stamped postcards in Europe and the U.S. respectively, 1893 and 1898 were crucial dates for the advance of private postcards in the United States, because it was not until the World Columbian Exposition in Chicago of 1893 that private postcards gained any popularity and notoriety. "…privately produced postcards did not come into general use until 1893, when thousands were sold as souvenirs of the World's Columbian Exposition in Chicago."[5]   Sales of postcards were linked to vacation visits to resorts or cities.

"…THE INFORMALITY OF THE POSTAL CARD ELIMINATED THE RIGID STRUCTURE OF THE LETTER. IT WAS EASIER AND MORE FUN TO SEND A POSTCARD. MUCH AS IN EUROPE, THE DIFFERENCE IN STYLE OF WRITING BETWEEN POSTCARDS AND LETTERS WAS OBVIOUS IN THE UNITED STATES."

In 1898 the U.S. government granted private postcards the same mailing privileges as the government issued cards. Rather than costing two cents to mail, the private postals now only cost one cent to mail. In addition, legislation required that the private cards have the same physical size and shape as the government issued cards. All private postals were also required to have *Private Mailing Card-Authorized by Act of Congress, May 19, 1898.*[6] In 1901 that message was shortened to Postcard. With this act the private postals had the same advantages as the government variety, and sales increased.

Another element of the postcard's popularity was related not to postcards themselves, but to the way in which the United States Postal Service functioned. Prior to 1906, only about twenty-five percent of the American population had the advantage of free home mail delivery. Those who did not live in a town of 10,000 or larger had to travel to the post office to receive mail. By 1906 Rural Free Delivery (RFD) ensured that the majority of homes and farms throughout the country received mail daily, and thus postcards became a common method of relaying brief messages. [7]

They announced births, weddings, visits and dinner invitations. At only one cent in postage, postcards were a pleasant and affordable means of sending word of visits. "In an era when few people traveled very far from home and few small town newspapers carried new photographs, buying a postcard depicting an event of local, national, or even international interest was a special and affordable treat…"[8] The decade prior to World War I was a grand one for the postal card. Cards commemorated everything from births to expositions and the ground breaking of new buildings.

Additionally, the informality of the postal card eliminated the rigid structure of the letter. It was easier and more fun to send a postcard. Much as in Europe, the difference in style of writing between postcards and letters was obvious in the United States. "The long descriptive phrases and lengthy expressions of endearment that had been common in letter writing gave way to the few terse phrases or sentences required for postcards."[9] Gentility and etiquette were sacrificed. The postcard became an easier more efficient, personalized method of communication. In an era of the rigid mannerisms of Victorian America, the postcard created a niche that had rules all its own. "A break with the traditional epistolary style in favor of a clipped new form of communication, postcard messages suited an age of speed and convenience…"[10]

Despite the fact that large companies sold a great number of postcards there was still room in the market for small producers. Entrepreneurs could easily try their luck at the postcard business thanks to the genius of George Eastman whose 1903 invention, the Kodak 3A camera, made it possible for almost any American to become an amateur photographer. The new model cost only two dollars and produced negatives just the size to make postcards. The ease and availability of new picture-making products meant the widespread commerce of pictures. Whether it was an amateur taking pictures at home, or a photographer making postcards, pictures became a commonplace product of the early twentieth century.

In 1907 new postal regulations made postcards with divided backs possible. Prior to that regulation only the address of the recipient was permissible on the back of the card. Personal messages had to be placed on the picture side of the card. Divided backs allowed for writing space that did not damage or intrude upon the picture on the front of the postcard. Postcards also reveal another trend that characterized this era, hometown or community boosterism, and it is this trend which so typifies the samples here from the Nina Heald Webber Southwest Colorado Postcard Collection at the Center of Southwest Studies on the Fort Lewis College campus. ◆

BIBLIOGRAPHY

Barrett, Terry. *Critizing Photographs: An Introduction to Understanding Images.* Mountain View, CA: Mayfield Publishing Company, 1990.

Burdick, J.R. *Pioneer Postcards.* 1957.

Klamkin, Marian. *Picture Postcards.* New York, NY: Dodd, Mead & Company, 1974.

Rosenblum, Naomi. *A World History of Photography.* New York, NY: Abbeville Publishers, 1989.

Schlereth, Thomas. *Victorian America 1876-1915.* New York, NY: Harper Collins Publishers, 1991.

Vanderwood and Samponaro. *Border Fury.* Albuquerque, NM: University of New Mexico Press, 1987.

ENDNOTES

[1] Marian Klamkin, *Picture Postcards* (New York, NY: Dodd, Mead & Company, 1974), p. 28.

[2] Ibid., p. 24.

[3] Ibid., p. 32.

[4] Thomas Schlereth, *Victorian America 1876-1915* (New York, NY: Harper Collins Publishers, 1991), p. 181.

[5] Vanderwood and Samponaro, *Border Fury* (Albuquerque, NM: University of New Mexico Press, 1987), p. 2.

[6] Ibid., p. 2.

[7] Ibid., p. 2.

[8] Ibid., p. 3.

[9] Ibid., p. 7.

[10] Ibid., p. 181.

APPENDIX B: THE PHENOMENON OF THE POSTCARD

BY TODD ELLISON

In the early days of America, philanthropists took ship and toured Europe, bringing home to U.S. museums an array of antiquities and fabulous works of classical art. Similarly, wealthy big-game hunters went on safari in Africa, obtaining their trophies of the hunt (now, they bring home photos instead of mounted animal heads). Then, with the advent of the automobile and the quintessentially American "love affair with the car" that began in the early twentieth century, middle-class citizens saw their country (and, sometimes, other countries) and bought postcards. Postcards rose in popularity along with the financial prosperity of the middle class. Countless millions of postcards have been sold. Postcard collecting is probably one of the top hobbies in the world, along with coins, stamps, and genealogical research.

It is understandable that postcards have been such a hit. They are affordable; they are colorful; they take up little space (either for the vendor, or for the end user); they are fairly easy to organize and to manage; and they document scenes that the amateur photographer would not be able to capture as effectively. Sometimes, they takes us to times and places we ourselves have not experienced. "The postcard allows the traveler to quickly share an image with family and friends, relate the enjoyment and the scenery, and wish them the same travel experience. No wonder 'Wish you were here' is the most universal postcard greeting."[1]

What motivates the postcard purchaser? "Wishing you were here" is a commonly expressed sentiment. Communication is a key function of the postcard — sending home a brief word and conveying a representation of something that has become part of the tourist's recent experience (even if the sum total of that experience was to pop into a store to buy the postcard). Perhaps postcards are a derivative of the collections of photographs that were popular in American homes in the 1860s. Cartes de visite and other photographic portrait cards were originally meant to replace the French calling cards left by genteel visitors.[2]

Postcards represent a truly American bent toward standardization that dates back to interchangeable parts for firearms and Henry Ford's Model T. As such, they represent an aspect of popular culture.

POSTCARDS HAVE TWO SIDES

Along with describing a scene, postcards offer a sidelong perspective on the millions of persons who bought them and mailed them to their friends and relatives.

To the researcher and to the postcard collector, this other side may be just as fascinating as the picture. The University of Delaware Library has noted in regard to its online collection of regional postcard images: "Postcards are not only visual records. Many of the postcards were in fact mailed and so contain written messages, stamps, and postmarks. The backs of the cards were also printed with information about the publisher, captions describing the image, and ornament. The printed text, along with the stamp and postmark, can help to date and place the manufacture and use of the cards. Alternatively, the captions and written messages contain a wealth of information that can be used to learn about the postcard's image or to illuminate the attitudes and interests of the past."[3]

WHAT POSTCARDS TEACH US ABOUT THE WEST

Postcards are especially useful as documentation of Western expansion across the North American continent. The University of Washington Libraries produced an exhibit entitled "'Hope to be there on Monday': the Postcard and the Western Traveler." The library displayed postcard images and messages along with tourists' snapshot photos and printed ephemera and souvenirs "to depict the changing role of tourism in the American West as the automobile became the major mode of travel. Among the prominent themes of the exhibit was American society's fascination with certain aspects of The West. The largest trees, the highest falls, the deepest canyons, the most colorful geothermal pots, the most convoluted and contorted landscapes: the West of the postcard was a phantasmagoria of nature."[4] So much of the American expansion into the vast spaces of the West occurred during the heyday of postcards, that the two phenomena developed hand in hand.

THE VALUE OF POSTCARDS FOR HISTORICAL RESEARCH

Postcards have preserved many millions of images of sites — some of which are no longer extant. As such, they can have genuine historical research value. History professor Scott Nelson was humming the folk ballad "John Henry" while studying a 1912 postcard of the Virginia State Penitentiary in Richmond, and made a connection between the view he was seeing and a cryptic line in the ballad "John Henry," a song referring to the brutality of railroad tunnel construction in the 1870s. "For decades," an article about Nelson noted, "the final stanza of "John Henry" has stumped historians: They took John Henry to the white house and they buried him in the sand/Now every locomotive that come roarin' by says there lies a steel-driving man." Nelson used the postcard of the white building at the penitentiary so that he "connected several important clues to determine that the folk hero was probably a convict who died while working on the Chesapeake & Ohio Railroad line in the 1870s and was buried on the grounds of the penitentiary." Nelson, a labor historian, presented his findings at the Social Science History Association Meeting in Chicago.[5]

As the University of Washington Libraries note in association with its large postcard collection, "As pieces of paper ephemera, postcards are frequently overlooked as sources of information or as a significant research tool, but their value is increasingly apparent. Postcards are not only illustrative, but, in quantity, they also serve as markers of popular taste and attitudes. Despite the obvious possibility of inauthenticity, postcards are often highly appealing because they provide the only image of a building or scene that is in color. … Examining the postcards of a town or city can pinpoint what features or characteristics were considered to be distinctive or valuable. Postcard publishers issued cards that would appeal to tourists. However, they also wanted them to interest the residents, who frequently mailed cards to friends and relatives who might never visit the place. Cards depicting public buildings, railroad stations, parks, were, in effect, benchmarks of civic achievement. They enabled both visitors and out-of-towners to see exactly how well their city compared with others." UW's Richard H. Engeman concludes, "Postcards are visual tidbits and pop culture touchstones, and they are documentations of small-town streets and local industries."[6]

SOME CONSIDERATIONS IN EVALUATING A POSTCARD AS A HISTORICAL DOCUMENT:

Consider the motivations for selling postcards. Postcard production is not, as a rule, a personal or a passionate enterprise. It is commercial. Postcards are designed for display in racks in stores where persons who have twenty seconds to "find a little something" will be able to drop a little cash to send home an image that will report on the trip.

Consider the process of producing a postcard. Postcards are not a product of spontaneity. An exception is some of the earlier black and white postcards which were actually photoprints printed on paper stamped as a postcard on the other side.

Some possible drawbacks of using postcards for historical research.
Postcards are apt to present an *artificial* representation of life. Seldom does a postcard depict the seedy or depressed side of a city. Seldom do the sentiments scribbled on the back tell the woes or hardships of the sender. Although postcards can reveal architectural and other details of the subjects pictured, they also speak volumes in terms of what is, in the congregate of postcards of a certain region, omitted.

The multiple dates of postcards.
Andrew J. Morris notes that "Knowing the dates associated with a postcard can make those bits of information more useful." Morris notes the various dates that are associated with any card: the date of the image's creation, of the card's manufacture, and of its use. He observes,

> *If we think of postcards as historic documents, then it is easy to see why the associated dates are important. A street scene for example, if the image date is known, can provide information about the buildings, infrastructure, and businesses in that part of town. Portraits can show how people dressed and some aspects of their behavior. Advertising cards can show how companies represented their products and services, which is a direct reflection of the values and customs of their age. Changes in the styles and subject matter of drawn illustrations can illustrate the changing tastes and esthetic judgments of their time. Picture postcards have captured the images of more than a century of changing material artifacts of civilization. They have recorded the faces and homes, business and environment from Alaska to Zanzibar. Nor is it just the historian who can benefit from the information, graphic and otherwise, found in postcards. Illustrators can get ideas and inspiration from the works of their predecessors, as well as from photographic images. The genealogist can learn more about the places their ancestors lived, as well as inscriptions from the most recent of those ancestors, or even pictures of the ancestors themselves. Authors writing on almost any subject may find illustrations that complement or enhance their texts.[7]*

It is possible to date postcards, at least approximately, by studying three types of clues they contain: the characteristic era of the style in which they were produced, the amount of postage required for their mailing, and the publisher's postcard numbering scheme. For information, see the Center of Southwest Studies' Web site at http://swcenter.fortlewis.edu/images/M194/PostcardDating.htm. Other clues in establishing the publication date are to study the picture, card, printing, and the use (or not) of telephone area codes and zip codes.

The inherent content of the picture may be helpful in dating (assuming that the postcard used a recent view). *The Official Identification and Price Guide to Postcards*[9] by Diane Allmen suggests looking at the following:

1. What style of **clothes** are the people wearing? A useful book in this regard is Joan Severa's *Dressed for the photographer: ordinary Americans and fashion, 1840-1900*.[10]

2. Look at the modes of **transportation**. Horse-drawn vehicles? Streetcars? What model of vehicles?

3. What clues can be drawn from the style of interior **decorations**, appliances, and furnishings? Technology can be a useful dating tool.

4. Have the buildings been **modified** since the time of this view? Dated photographs in other collections may be useful for comparing with the postcard view.

5. Look for other time-related **details**. For example, how many stars are in the U.S. flag? Do the buildings have window air conditioners? Is a wall calendar in the picture?

As Allmen notes, **postcard size** can also be a clue to its date of origin.

■ If the card is old and is larger than 3.5 by 5.5 inches, it may date from before 1898.

■ If the card is old and is slightly smaller than 3.5 by 5.5 inches, it may date from 1898-1902.

■ If the card measures 3.5 by 5.5 inches, it was probably made between 1902 and 1970.

■ If the card measures approximately 4 by 6 inches ("continental" size) and is American, it was probably made no earlier than the 1960s.

Allmen also suggests looking at the **printing process.**

■ If the card was produced using high-quality chromolithography with <u>six or more inks</u>, it was probably made before 1917.

■ If the card has a <u>flat-textured surface</u> and is printed with a <u>limited range of low-contrast inks</u>, it was probably made before 1930.

■ If it has a <u>linen-textured surface</u> and is printed with <u>sharply contrasting bright inks</u>, it is likely from the period 1930-1960.

■ If the card has a <u>shiny surface</u> and is printed in <u>color</u> using a <u>halftone</u> process (little dots of magenta, cyan, yellow and black), it was probably made no earlier than 1939.

Allmen observes that "postcards created directly from photographic negatives and printed onto photographic paper are difficult to date when they have not been postally used." She refers the user to two resources in this regard: *Prairie Fires and Paper Moons* by Hal Morgan and Andreas Brown (Boston: David R. Godine, 1981) and "Dating Post-1920 Real Photo Postcards," by Ernest G. Covington, in *Postcard Collector*, July 1986, pp. 26-28.

COLLECTING POSTCARDS TODAY

Today, a "traveler" can email an electronic postcard, with message attached, without leaving the home computer. Sites allow the sender to "mail" an aerial view of a city in Italy, with a message. You can even send yourself a postcard. It arrives within a second. It lacks much descriptive detail about the subject pictured, but it is free, pretty, convenient, and immediate. The Library of Congress and other libraries sell reproductions of postcards in their collections. The Web has fabulously benefited persons who are buying and selling postcards. Low-resolution images of such a relatively small picture are easily transmitted electronically. Web auction sites, notably eBay!, have been a boon for postcard sellers and collectors. Truly, the postcard has found its match in the Web. The University of Texas at Arlington, home of a sizeable postcard collection, has noted that "Postcard collecting is still very much part of our popular culture. There are local, national, and international postcard collecting organizations that sponsor annual shows for buying, selling, and showing every imaginable type of postcard. ... Postcards preserve memories of travels, but interests vary. People tend to specialize in collecting a type of postcard or a particular subject. For whatever reason, it becomes a passion."[14]

THE NINA HEALD WEBBER SOUTHWEST COLORADO POSTCARD COLLECTION AT THE CENTER OF SOUTHWEST STUDIES

One person for whom postcard collecting has become a passion is Nina Heald Webber. Mrs. Webber's collection of Southwest Colorado postcards contains more than two thousand postcards of Durango, Silverton, Ouray, Telluride and adjacent areas, which she loaned to the Center of Southwest Studies for digitization. The generosity and thoughtfulness of this donor in lending items so that they can be broadly appreciated is an example of a direction in which cultural repositories can move, thanks to the benefits of technology. Funding for the center's digitization and online image access project was provided by Colorado Digitization Program (CDP) grants as part of a multi-state Collaborative Digitization Program. CDP projects are supported through a National Leadership Grant from the Institute of Museum and Library Services (a federal grant-making agency in Washington, D.C., which fosters innovation, leadership and a lifetime of learning by supporting museums and libraries) with additional assistance from the Colorado State Library and the Colorado Regional Library Systems. The Southwest Center, for its part, has invested thousands of staff hours and thousands of dollars to catalog each postcard and make each one accessible on the Web for researcher viewing. The home page is http://swcenter.fortlewis.edu/inventory/PostcardsInv.htm. The center considered it important to provide access to both sides of each postcard, because of the research value of the non-picture side of a card.

This three-part venture of the donor, the funding source, and the cultural repository is serving as a model for preserving traces of a region's history that otherwise would be unavailable. One of many benefits of the accessibility of this collection is that the postcards provide historical preservation specialists with an invaluable resource used when restoring old buildings in the Southwest. For example, a team of researchers found them useful for a restoration project in Telluride. The center expects to maintain and support the use of these digital images and Web pages, because they serve a role in connecting researchers with a picture of the past. All of this fulfills the mission of the Center of Southwest Studies: to connect individuals with the history and culture of the Southwest. ◆

[1] *Wish I Were There: The Jenkins Garrett Postcard Collection, 1903-1996,* The Compass Rose, Special Collections Division, the University of Texas at Arlington Libraries, Vol. XIII * No. 1 * Spring 1999, web page viewed on 2/19/2004 at http://libraries.uta.edu/SpecColl/crose99/postcard.htm. The site lists as its sources for the article, Diane Allmen, *The Official Identification and Price Guide to Postcards.* New York: House of Collectibles, 1990; and H. Martin Seward. "A Short History of the Picture Postcard," a paper presented at the Texas State Historical Association meeting, March 2, 1996.

[2] For an excellent brief history of the postcard, see *Wish I Were There: The Jenkins Garrett Postcard Collection, 1903-1996,* The Compass Rose, Special Collections Division, the University of Texas at Arlington Libraries, Vol. XIII * No. 1 * Spring 1999, web page viewed on 2/19/2004 at http://libraries.uta.edu/SpecColl/crose99/postcard.htm The site lists as its sources for the article, Diane Allmen, *The Official Identification and Price Guide to Postcards.* New York: House of Collectibles, 1990; and H. Martin Seward. "A Short History of the Picture Postcard," a paper presented at the Texas State Historical Association meeting, March 2, 1996.

[3] "About the Collection," University of Delaware Library Web site viewed at http://www.lib.udel.edu/digital/dpc/ on 2/19/2004.

"'Greetings from the Country': the University of Washington Libraries Postcard Collection," Special Collections, University of Washington, viewed on 2/19/2004 at http://www.lib.washington.edu/specialcoll/collections/postcard/postcard.html

[4] "History Professor Locates Gravesite Of Folk Hero: Postcard yields clues about John Henry's final days," *The William & Mary News,* December 10, 1998, Web page viewed on 2/19/2004 at http://www.wm.edu/wmnews/121098/henry.html

[5] "'Greetings from the Country': the University of Washington Libraries Postcard Collection," Special Collections, University of Washington, Web page viewed on 2/19/2004 at http://www.lib.washington.edu/specialcoll/collections/postcard/postcard.html For additional information by the same author, see "Pacific Northwest and Other Post card Treasures in the University of Washington Libraries," by Richard H. Engeman, in *Postcards in the Library: Invaluable Visual Resources,* edited by Norman D. Stevens (Haworth Press, 1995); also published as Popular Culture in Libraries, vol. 3, #2 (1995).

[6] For a wealth of tips on dating postcards, see the Center of Southwest Studies'

Web site at http://swcenter.fortlewis.edu/images/M194/PostcardDating.htm. Much of the contents of these guidelines were excerpted with permission from the *Beginner's Guide to the Hobby of Postcard Collecting*, The Capital of Texas Postcard Club, http://communitylink.austin360.com/groups/084/FSLO-1017493573-307084.doc (site no longer active as of 2/19/2004). Other sites with helpful tips for dating postcards are: http://www.ajmorris.com/roots/photo/postcard/how.htm and http://bibliomania.net/gruetzcards.html ("A Brief Guide to Identifying and Dating Postcards in the US").

[7] Andrew J. Morris, "Dating Postcards - Why Bother?" Web page viewed at http://www.ajmorris.com/roots/photo/postcard/index.htm on 2/19/2004.

[8] Diane Allmen, *The Official Identification and Price Guide to Postcards (New York: House of Collectibles)*, 1990, ISBN 0-876-37802-5, p. 16.

[9] Kent, Ohio: Kent State University Press, 1995.

[10] Allmen, p. 17-18.

[11] Allmen, p. 18.

[12] Allmen, p. 19.

[13] *Wish I Were There: The Jenkins Garrett Postcard Collection, 1903-1996*, The Compass Rose, Special Collections Division, the University of Texas at Arlington Libraries, Vol. XIII * No. 1 * Spring 1999, viewed on 2/19/2004 at http://libraries.uta.edu/SpecColl/crose99/postcard.htm The site lists as its sources for the article, Diane Allmen, *The Official Identification and Price Guide to Postcards*. New York: House of Collectibles, 1990; and H. Martin Seward. "A Short History of the Picture Postcard," a paper presented at the Texas State Historical Association meeting, March 2, 1996.

ABOUT THE EDITOR:

ANDREW GULLIFORD is a professor of Southwest Studies and History and Director of the Center of Southwest Studies at Fort Lewis College in Durango, Colorado where he coordinates a minor in Heritage Preservation and directs the $8 million, 48,000-square-foot Center of Southwest Studies. His books include *Boomtown Blues: Colorado Oil Shale, America's County Schools, Sacred Objects* and *Sacred Places: Preserving Tribal Traditions*, and in 2005 the University of New Mexico Press will publish his edited book *Preserving Western History: Public History and Historic Preservation in the American West*. Dr. Gulliford leads tours of the American West for the Smithsonian Institution and the National Trust for Historic Preservation. He has been appointed to the National Register Review Board for the State of Colorado and to the Bureau of Land Management's Resource Advisory Council for southwest Colorado.

ABOUT THE AUTHORS:

LYNNE CARPENTER received her B.A. in American History from Seattle University in Seattle, Washington in 1994, her M.A in American Studies from the University of Wyoming in 1997, and her Masters in Teaching in 1998 from Seattle University. Currently, she is completing her sixth year of teaching English, history, and Spanish at the eighth grade level in Oak Harbor, Washington. Her passions include teaching, the study of western authors, and travel to places like Africa, Spain, and Venezuela. Lynne believes the American West is a place whose mythic and real histories should reside in the hearts of all, that they, and it, be preserved for posterity. She lives and learns on Whidbey Island in Northwest Washington.

TODD ELLISON is the Fort Lewis College Archivist and a Professor in the Libraries. He practices and teaches all aspects of archives and records management. Ellison has been on the staff of the Center of Southwest Studies since establishing the college's archives in 1991. His B.A. in history is from Middlebury College, and his two masters degrees at the University of Maryland focused on archival work. Ellison has 20 years of experience as a leader in a broad range of archival work, including pioneering work in the late 1980s at the Boulder (Colo.) Public Library, which became the first library in the U.S. to have its historic photos viewable on a public access catalog. The only Certified Archivist in southwest Colorado, he is a member of the Society of American Archivists and the Society of Rocky Mountain Archivists. He has produced 100 guides to the Special Collections at the Center of Southwest Studies, and nearly 100 special collections forms for use, to regulate the access and management of the collections at the Center.

ART GOODTIMES is a 25-year resident of the San Miguel Basin Watershed on the Western Slope of Colorado, a small landowner on Wright's Mesa, non-commercial grower of 35 varieties of organic heirloom seed potatoes (Cloud Acre Spuds), former private school Latin teacher, husband and parent, and remains self-employed as a performance poet, newspaper columnist and festival director, as well as serving as an elected Green county commissioner.

ANN HOFFMAN enjoyed living her formative years in Ignacio, Colorado, and spent many happy summer hours at points along the western slope from Ouray's Amphitheatre to the Grand Mesa near Grand Junction. She has been an avid hiker and jeeper in the San Juan Mountains of Ouray and San Juan Counties. Ann was one of the founders of the Red Mountain Task Force/Red Mountain Project. She has participated in the Project's efforts to save the scenic and recreational landscape of the Red Mountain Mining District and its significant historical structures from modern development. In 1992 she retired from a forty-year career in nursing, having degrees in nursing and education. She, and her husband Neil, settled near Ouray. They have enjoyed many happy hours with friends, and their four children and spouses, and eight grandchildren. In late 1997, Ann accepted the challenge of Executive Director at the Ouray County Historical Society and its Museum. Recently she retired after nearly seven years of service to the community and visitors worldwide.

NIK KENDZIORSKI received his B.A. degree in history from Kalamazoo College in Michigan and his M.A. degree in American Studies from the University of Wyoming. A Western historian who consults on properties for the National Register of Historic Places, Nik has hiked and explored in Hawai'i, California, Wyoming, New Mexico and Colorado. In California he supervised three historic properties for the San Diego Historical Society, and in Hawai'i he supervised high school students on special visits to the sacred island Kahoolawe. An avid skier, snowshoer, hiker, and historical interpreter, Nik is thoroughly familiar with the San Juan Mountains of southwest Colorado and the Weminuche Wilderness as well as La Plata Canyon, the Four-Wheel Drive Alpine Loop, Mesa Verde National Park, Chaco Culture National Historical Park and the newly designated Canyons of the Ancients National Monument. He lives near Durango with his wife Amy, an assistant principal, and his son Andrew.

RICHARD MOE graduated from Williams College in 1959 and soon launched the public-service career that led to the chairmanship of the Minnesota Democratic-Farmer-Labor Party. He also earned a law degree from the University of Minnesota Law School. In 1972 he moved to Washington, D.C. to be administrative assistant to Senator Walter F. Mondale. Five years later he was named chief of staff to Vice President Mondale and a member of the Carter White House senior staff. He practiced law in Washington from 1981 until he became the seventh president of the National Trust for Historic Preservation in 1993. Chartered by Congress in 1949, the National Trust is the largest nonprofit preservation organization in the United States. A member of the Committee for the Preservation of the White House and the boards of the Ford Foundation and the Civil War Trust, Moe was awarded an honorary doctorate from the University of Maryland in 1998 that recognized his work in the field of historic preservation. He is co-author of *Changing Places: Rebuilding Community in the Age of Sprawl* and *The Last Full Measure: The Life and Death of the First Minnesota Volunteers*, a Civil War history.

FREDA CARLEY PETERSON — After attending high school and McPherson College in McPherson, Kansas, she was, from 1953 until 1990, Co-Founder, Vice-President and Manager of Oklahoma's Oil-Law Records Corporation. In the 1970s she became interested in the history of Silverton, Colorado, purchased and subsequently read (for eight years) all the microfilmed newspapers for San Juan County. Those records dated back to 1879. The result of her research was the monumental two-volume *The Story of Hillside Cemetery*, a demographic study which, in an earlier version, received a prestigious award (1990) from the American Association for State and Local History. This work is the only comprehensive biographical record documenting over 3,000 San Juan County, Colorado burials. Portions of this work have also appeared under the titles of *Over My Dead Body*, *Where Daisies Nod*, *Death in the Snow*, and *Faces of the Flu: The 1918 Epidemic in Silverton, Colorado*. All proceeds from these book sales are donated to the Hillside Cemetery Fund, which she and the San Juan County Historical Society established. As Chairman of the Society's Cemetery Committee, she supervises the $45,000 Cemetery Endowment.

BEVERLY RICH is a native of Silverton, daughter of a miner, and lover of the mountains. She is the San Juan County Treasurer, an elected position and a graduate of Fort Lewis College. In her spare time she is Chairman of the San Juan County Historical Society, a volunteer position. As Chairman of the historical society, she has brought several millon dollars of preservation funds into Silverton and San Juan County, where she has worked on projects such as the Silverton Town Hall Restoration and the Old 100 Boardinghouse Stabilization. As a child, she used to sell rocks (mineral specimens) to the tourists when the narrow-gauge trains came into town. Bev Rich has been very active in Colorado Preservation, Inc. and she serves on the board of advisors for the National Historic Landmarks Stewards Association. Rich has also served on the State Historical Fund Advisory Board and the Red Mountain Task Force. Thanks to her guidance Silverton has received national awards for historic preservation.

DUANE SMITH received his academic degrees from the University of Colorado and completed his Ph.D. in 1964. That year he began to teach at Fort Lewis College where he is a Professor of Southwest Studies. His areas of research and writing include Colorado history, Civil War history, mining history, urban history and baseball history. He is an extremely popular professor at Fort Lewis, and he is the author of over thirty books on a variety of subjects including *Rocky Mountain Mining Camps: The Urban Frontier*; *A Colorado History*; *Horace Tabor: His Life and the Legend*; *Silver Saga: The Story of Caribou Colorado*; *Colorado Mining: A Photographic History*; *Fortunes Are for the Few: Letters of a Forty-niner*; *Rocky Mountain Boom Town: A History of Durango*; *A Land Alone: Colorado's Western Slope*; *Song of the Hammer and Drill: The Colorado San Juans, 1860-1914*; *Mining America: The Industry and the Environment, 1800-1980*; *Mesa Verde National Park: Shadows of the Centuries*; *The Birth of Colorado: A Civil War Perspective*; and *Sacred Trust: The Birth and Development of Fort Lewis College*.

ABOUT THE DESIGNER:

LISA SNIDER ATCHISON is a freelance graphic designer and illustrator. She grew up in Salt Lake City, Utah. There she attended the University of Utah, where she received a B.F.A. in graphic design. Her design and illustration experience includes work with an advertising agency, illustrations for a children's book and a 3-year stint as staff artist at *The Durango Herald*. She received four first place Colorado Press Association awards for page design and informational graphics while at the *Herald*. Lisa moved to the Durango area in 1995. She enjoys mountain biking, hiking and snowshoeing. She loves to read and is an enthusiastic gardener. Most of all she enjoys the quiet and solitude of rural life. Lisa and her husband live, work and play with their daughter in the beautiful Pine River Valley.